Route Irish

Written by Paul Laverty
Directed by Ken Loach

route

First published in 2011 by Route
PO Box 167, Pontefract, WF8 4WW
info@route-online.com
www.route-online.com

In association with Sixteen Films
2nd Floor, 187 Wardour Street, London, W1F 8ZB

© Screenplay: Paul Laverty

ISBN: 978-1-901927-47-4

© Photographs: Joss Barratt

Cover design:
GOLDEN www.wearegolden.co.uk
from artwork supplied by Artificial Eye

Printed by CPI Antony Rowe

Route is supported by Arts Council England

Contents

Introduction   7
Paul Laverty

Fergus and Frankie   11
Backstory

Route Irish   19
Screenplay

Aftermath   151
Mark Townsend

Private Security Contractors in Iraq: 165
the lifeline of neo-colonial rule
Haifa Zangana

Justice for Iraq   181
Mike Phipps

Production Notes   195
Ken Loach, Rebecca O'Brien,
Mark Womack, Andrea Lowe

Film Credits   201

Introduction

Paul Laverty

We are all familiar with the ritual of the body of a dead soldier returning from foreign soil: solemn music, the national flag, escorts and salutes recorded in detail by the nation's media. Words of consolation flow from politicians and generals to broken-hearted relatives, many so young they often clutch infants. It wasn't quite that way for Deely, the sister of Robert, an ex-paratrooper who was ambushed in Iraq. He was flown back from Kuwait and arrived at Glasgow airport. The undertaker told Deely there were ten bodies on the plane that day, two of which were unidentifiable. Robert's coffin looked 'like a big orange crate'. There was no fanfare, no Union Jack, no journalists and not one question. His death, as far as we know, wasn't added to any list. The reason is simple. Robert was no longer a paratrooper, but a private contractor. Some call them private soldiers, or corporate warriors, or security consultants. Iraqis call them mercenaries.

The business of war is being privatised slowly and deliberately before our eyes. Robert's orange crate of a coffin tells us so, as do the statistics. Patrick Cockburn, a well-respected commentator on Iraq, estimated that there were around 160,000 foreign contractors in Iraq at the height of the occupation, many of whom – perhaps as many as 50,000 – were heavily armed security personnel. The conduct of the war, and occupation afterwards, would have been impossible without their muscle.

Thanks to Paul Bremer, the US appointed head of the Coalition Provisional Authority, each and every one of those contractors was given immunity from Iraqi law in the shape of Order 17 which was imposed on the new Iraqi Parliament. (Order 17 lasted from 2003 till the beginning of 2009.)

Nobody is interested in counting how many Iraqi civilians have been killed or injured by private contractors, but there is a vast body of evidence to suggest that there has been widespread abuse. Blackwater's massacre of seventeen civilians in the middle of Baghdad was the most notorious incident, but there were many more that went unreported. One senior contractor told me, on condition of anonymity, that he spoke to a South African who told him killing an Iraqi was just like 'shooting a Kafir'. Other bona fide contractors, proud of their professionalism, told me of their disgust at the violence of 'the cowboys'. If a contractor was involved in an incident which caused a fuss, they were whisked out of the country by their company. Impunity, by order.

While lowly contractors gambled with lives and limbs on Route Irish, the chief executives of those same companies made fortunes. Mr David Lesar, chief executive of Halliburton, (former CEO being Dick Cheney) earned just under 43 million dollars in 2004. Mr Gene Ray of Titan earned over 47 million between 2004 and 2005. Mr JP London of CACI earned 22 million. The devil is always in the detail. Private contractors charged the US army up to 100 dollars to do a single soldier's laundry bag. In an official report dated January 2005, the Special Investigator General for Iraq Reconstruction, Stuart Bowen, revealed that over 9 billion dollars had disappeared in fraud and corruption, and that was only during a very limited period of the Provisional Authority. Financial impunity too.

As one contractor told me, the 'place stank of money'. Little wonder that poorly paid soldiers and elite Special Forces left in such numbers to join these private military corporations, as they saw their chance of a lifetime 'to load up'.

These men 'load up' with more than cash.

We are now used to seeing images of carnage and slaughter 'over there'. We are accustomed to stories of missing billions, corporate greed, abuse, torture, and secret prisons. *The Lancet's* detailed estimate of 654,965 dead as at June 2006 is almost beyond the mind's capacity to grasp. It all seems now at a safe distance in time and place. Iraq fatigue, we are told, is upon us.

But 'over there' is on its way back home. Iraq is inside the heads of 'our boys'.

I was stunned to learn from the charity Combat Stress, who deal with ex-soldiers suffering from post-traumatic stress disorder, that on average it takes approximately fourteen years for PTSD to manifest itself. They are bracing themselves (as is the US army) for a massive surge in the years to come.

Norma, a gentle nurse on the point of retiring who had spent years with ex-soldiers, opened the way for this story when she told me 'many of these men are in mourning for their former selves'. An ex-soldier showed me a painting he had done of himself: 'I just want my old self back.'

Order 17 may have been revoked in Iraq but its spirit still reigns supreme: the stink of impunity, the lies, the contempt for international law, the undermining of the Geneva conventions, the secret prisons, the torture, the murder… the hundreds of thousands of dead. As I imagine the intellectual authors of the above, Bush, Blair, Rumsfeld and co., collecting their millions in after-dinner speeches and setting up their interfaith foundations, I cannot help but think of the nurses in Fallujah assisting the births of babies born with two heads and deformed faces thanks to the chemical bombs rained on that city. Our gift to the future.

So we wondered about Order 17 back home.

Iraq, in an English country garden.

Fergus and Frankie
Backstory

Fergus and Frankie were closest of mates from their first day at school in Liverpool.

Fergus had a chaotic childhood and adolescence peppered with trouble. He has long since lost contact with his father whom he barely remembers from childhood. His father worked on the ships as a merchant seaman. He has had very little contact with his mother too since she left for London after her second marriage when Fergus was just fifteen. The new husband wanted nothing to do with a troublesome out of control teenager. Fergus moved in with an aunt in Liverpool (since dead) who treated him as a burden. Any semblance of normal home life he had was with Frankie and Frankie's mother, who was very kind to him, and realised how close the two boys were.

Fergus applied to join the paras aged nineteen. Not for the first time Frankie followed him, and they joined together in the same intake.

Fergus and Frankie.
1990: They join the paras.
1991: Fermanagh.
1993–95: Belfast.
1996–97: South Armagh.

Fergus had a more impetuous side and was attracted to taking a chance. He wanted a new challenge and fresh excitement. He applied to join the SAS. Only 18 out of 180 completed the gruelling six-month course and he gets badged for SAS in January 2000.

Meanwhile, Frankie, more cautious, is reluctant to leave the paras. He is steady, fair, comic, and becomes a very popular and respected sergeant.

In 2001 both the paras and SAS are sent out to Macedonia where their paths occasionally crossed. The dispute in Afghanistan heats up. Frankie is sent out with the paras from December 2001 and stays until April 2002. Fergus is sent out there too from October 2001 to January 2002.

May 2002: During a break back home Fergus meets Rachel in a gym. There is an immediate visceral connection. In another time they would have ended up together, without doubt. But it is not for the first time in her life that Rachel has been attracted to 'difficult and complicated' men. She gave up her college course – sports science at a Liverpool college – to follow a troublesome musician around Europe, and stayed with him for far too long. Perhaps there have been a few more relationships of a similar nature. After a crisis in her life she is determined not to repeat the mistakes of the past, and now really wants to get her life in order, both professionally and privately. She experimented with too many drugs (dope, Es and maybe cocaine, but not heroin) and it has taken her time to get back on an even keel. She is tired of the anxiousness, paranoia and sense of drift in her life. Time to focus. She wants to make a career in fitness and health (which has been her way of getting back on track) and is determined to open her own studio. Her sense of time lost adds bite to her ambition.

On a night out Fergus introduces her to Frankie. There is something 'big' about him in every way. He is at ease with himself – the source of his confidence. He seems generous and makes her laugh. He is organised, tough, and lets it drop that he would love to have kids one day. This is an issue for her too with the biological clock ticking. He is the type of man that would make her feel safe when she gets anxious. After they meet up again at a half marathon Fergus spots their connection.

Fergus backs off and leaves Frankie and Rachel to get on with it. But there is a deep current of sometimes contradictory emotion between the three. Fergus and Frankie broached the subject one night during a drinking session, after which they both got 'Rachel' tattooed on their arms.

Frankie goes to South Armagh in 2002 and leaves the army in July 2003 to be with Rachel who wants him home.

Frankie struggles to find work he likes. They decide to save every penny to open their own studio, and in the meantime he works as a bailiff in some of the toughest parts of Liverpool.

While he is still madly in love with Rachel he misses the life of a soldier, and misses his mate Fergus more than anyone.

Fergus goes to Iraq – between December 2003 and April 2004 – with the SAS and carries out joint operations in search of 'terrorists' with his US counterparts in Special Forces. Both groups are based in old villas near the Tigris which once belonged to senior Baathists.

Fergus becomes disillusioned with what he has seen and done and leaves the regiment in May 2004 after a conversation with Haynes, an ex-officer, who has terrific contacts and headhunts elite forces for his own private security company which is booming in post-invasion Iraq. Fergus joins Haynes almost immediately at the end of May 2004.

On a break back home, in August 2004, he persuades Frankie to join his team and work with Haynes too. (Rachel was very confused by Frankie's decision to go to Iraq. Frankie told her he would only work with top professionals with a track record. No cowboys. Her way of dealing with the terrible danger was to avoid thinking about it as much as possible, as Frankie promised not to take any chances, and to come back home if he felt it was getting too dangerous. And of course, at ten grand a month, within eighteen months they would have enough capital to open up their own studio, and have a great start on their life together. Without acknowledging it she realised how much Frankie was missing Fergus too, and how he was constantly following his progress in Iraq. Fergus also promised her he'd look after him – they always had looked after each other in Ireland. They would do so again in Iraq.)

By June 2005 Fergus has established friendships with many of the businessmen working from the Green Zone who have come to rely on him for their safety. They appreciated his intelligence and authority, and enjoy his witty company. He is fascinated by the cut and thrust of the expanding opportunities and, after being in the forces, totally stunned at the amount of money on offer. He soon realises anything Haynes can do, he can do. If he is taking all the chances, why shouldn't he do it for himself? He'd seen enough of the officer class in the forces.

For some time he had been cultivating his own contacts in the Green Zone, but in June 2005 he is offered a golden opportunity to provide security for a huge site with many foreign workers and takes the chance with both hands. He undercuts and dumps Haynes and sets up his own private company hiring many of the Colombians and Iraqi guards he has got to know over the previous year. This suits the new contractor, Fergus, but infuriates Haynes.

Fergus has worked like a dog since June 2005 but after the first seven months due to the volume of work he has begun to cut corners. Work, enormous pressure, great danger, and a few close shaves have begun to take their toll. At the beginning of December 2006 Fergus loses three of his men and the pressure mounts. He saved his client, but left his men behind which goes deeply against the grain.

These deaths and a narrow escape bring back deeply disturbing memories, especially one that he has tried to bury: Fergus, during his time with the SAS, was a witness to the aftermath of an Allied bombing of a suspected terrorist house which went all wrong. He saw a grandfather pull a child with a lilac dress and shredded leg from the rubble of their home. In moments of stress she often points at him as he tries to sleep.

After losing his men Fergus has had great difficulty sleeping. There is a sense of crisis and emptiness in his life.

Fergus sells his business to an old mate from the SAS for a greatly reduced fee – to oversee and keep the existing contracts in order till their expiration – and heads back to Liverpool and his new apartment for Christmas 2006. But he can barely stand the place and more often than not takes refuge with his blind mate Craig, an old mate from the paras who was badly injured as a contractor in Iraq.

The first months of 2007 have passed in a daze, with far too many drinking bouts, and then desperate attempts to get himself back in shape again. He is too embarrassed to meet up with Rachel, although he thinks of her often. He makes excuses whenever she phones him. Although she thinks of Frankie too, Fergus often comes to mind. She recognises his self-destructive streak, something she understands from her own life.

In September 2007 he seriously assaults bouncers who have insulted Craig and laughed at his condition. He doesn't really understand his own fury, far less deal with it. He is forced to give up his passport as he awaits trial.

Meanwhile in Iraq, Frankie too has been struggling with the stress of the job, and greatly misses Fergus. (Even though they have worked in different companies, they kept close contact.)

On 17 September 2007 Fergus's world falls apart as Frankie dies.

But the shock gives him determination to focus again and find out what happened. He feels a terrible sense of grief – like losing a brother and soul mate. He also carries a tremendous responsibility after persuading him to join him in Iraq. His sense of fury grows too once he realises they are hiding something. He wants justice for his soul mate – but vengeance lurks there too. There is no way he can delegate the investigation to the police. Questions dominate every moment of his life. The whole Iraq experience weighs upon him, and the death of Frankie is the last straw.

He is drawn to the Mersey and the ferry – to youthful memories with Frankie, and all their plans for the future. He keeps wrestling with a deep undercurrent, and desperately tries to capture 'how they were'. He wouldn't put it in these terms, but Rachel is the only one who really knows; perhaps that is why all three are tangled up so completely. Fergus has lost Frankie, the love of his life.

Route Irish
Screenplay

1. FERRY BOAT, LIVERPOOL

Fergus stares into the choppy waters below. His eyes are red, and he is deeply upset. He closes his eyes, and remembers.

CUT TO A BLACK SCREEN:

A rugged male voice leaves multiple messages on an answering machine; the intensity deepens after each click.

TITLES:

ROUTE IRISH
[LIVERPOOL 2007]

VOICE OVER

Hey… Cuntylugs! Frankie here… Where are
you? Give me a call. [Click] Hey Dick Head…
did you get my message on your mobile?…
Phone me back… this is an order! [Click]
Fergus… Come on man… I'm getting tired of
this… midnight your time… phone me when
you get in… doesn't matter how late… I'll still
be up counting the stars… got to speak mate.
[Click. Another, now much more serious]
Fergus… Are you on the piss again? I really
need to speak to you… phone me…

BACK TO THE FERRY: FERGUS, [late thirties, brawny, casually dressed but with expensive good taste] still stands by the railing on the upper deck of the ferry which crosses between Birkenhead and Liverpool. He looks out towards the estuary and horizon beyond as the messages continue to haunt his mind. He takes a sip from an open bottle of wine he grips by the neck.

> VOICE OVER (CONT'D)
> [Click. Now urgent] Fergus… [pause]… Fuck!
> I need you man! I need you now! Not
> tomorrow… Now! Fucking phone me! I'm all
> mixed up… [deep frustration] Just piss off!…
> useless fucking waster… [pause, resigned]…
> Phone me when you can Fergus… I'm up
> against it here… [struggling and sense of
> panic] I don't know what to do man… I really
> don't know what to fucking do… need your
> help mate… I need you… I need you Fergus…

Fergus, distressed, turns from the horizon and stares out over the empty deck of the ferry… his mind drifts back twenty years.

UPPER DECK OF ANOTHER FERRY: [As if a dreamlike state – black and white.] Two handsome fifteen-year-olds, Fergus and mate FRANKIE [big, powerful], horse around on the top deck. Fergus, gripping a bottle of Buckfast, jumps onto Frankie's back.

> FRANKIE
> Fergus! You skinny bastard… off me back!

He spins him round in circles.

FERGUS

Take me to New York!

Frankie charges to the bow of the ship with Fergus's legs dangling at each side of Frankie's broad frame. They giggle and joke as they look out to the horizon.

CUT to Fergus, the man, now, at the railing.

FERGUS (CONT'D)

[Whispered to himself] Oh Frankie…

He turns from the empty deck, and hurls the bottle with a ferocious energy towards the horizon.

2. CATHOLIC CHURCH, LIVERPOOL

Fergus, dressed in an impeccable black suit, pushes open a door leading into the special quiet and enchanting gloom of an old church. He peers from the back and stares at the coffin in front of the altar. Mourners kneel and say silent prayers.

RACHEL, a young woman, pale faced, [skinny but in an athletic kind of way] turns and catches sight of him. She's already marching towards him. Fergus knows what's coming. Rachel pounds his shoulder with a full-blooded blow. They stare at each other's pain. Fergus looks to the ground. There are no words. She marches out.

Fergus moves towards the coffin. He spots the undertaker by the side aisle and moves quickly towards him.

FERGUS

[Whisper] I've got to see Frankie…

UNDERTAKER

[Taken aback] I'm very sorry Sir… not even

his family have seen him... [still not enough]...
the coffin has been sealed.

FERGUS

When everyone leaves... I'll see him then.

The undertaker is shocked by the look in his eye.

UNDERTAKER

Sorry Sir... you don't understand... it's for the
best... he's not really... complete...

Frankie steps far too close for comfort as the undertaker's
alarm grows.

FERGUS

[Still a whisper] I'm not asking you... I'm
telling you...

UNDERTAKER

I'm very sorry...

He backs off quickly and scuttles out.

Fergus moves to the coffin. He lays his hand upon it and can
see his own fingers tremble.

OUTSIDE THE CHURCH: The last couple of mourners
leave.

BACK INSIDE THE CHURCH: Lights are switched off. The
coffin sits there in dim isolation before the altar. From behind a
pillar Fergus peers at the Sacristan who is locking up the main
door and then exits.

Now total silence. Fergus approaches the altar. He stares at the
coffin and then checks around once more. He takes out a crow
bar from inside his jacket. He jams the instrument under the

lid. The cracking wood sounds horribly violent in this space. He heaves, and the lid breaks loose. He lifts it off.

He stares for a long moment as he tries to control his grief.

                    FERGUS
        Not a tie Frankie… [He leans in and takes it
        off] You always hated ties man… that's
        better… much better…

He dangles the tie round his own neck as he stares down at his mate.

After a moment Fergus takes Frankie's hand from inside the coffin and cradles it in his own. [That's all we see of Frankie's body.]

                    FERGUS (CONT'D)
        At least I recognise your hands Frankie… How
        did this happen? Eh? Get up Frankie… get up
        and let's go… right now… get up I said you
        lazy bastard! Rachel's out there… she's waiting
        for you… [Almost a wail] Oh Christ… I
        should have been watching your back
        Frankie… looking after you… the way you
        looked after me… always… [Pause, losing
        control] Oh Frankie… I can't fucking bear
        this…

He kisses Frankie's hand and carefully places it inside the coffin again.

                    FERGUS (CONT'D)
        Should have been me…

3. CHURCH – NEXT MORNING

Bright sunlight streams in through the windows.

Mourners are already seated. Besides family many are in soldiers' uniform and even more are well-built men in civilian clothes. Clearly many of them are ex-military. A few are in wheelchairs. Fergus sits beside his friend CRAIG who is blind and holds a white stick. [His face has been deeply marked by shrapnel.]

The church sound system rings with the emotional sounds of Verdi's 'Chorus of Hebrew Slaves'.

As the music continues the sombre faces of family and friends – many with crew cuts – stare towards the altar. [It appears strange – but a half dozen or so catch each other's eyes, and whistle silently to the same music.]

Fergus and Craig [silently whistling too] sit a few rows behind Rachel and the rest of Frankie's family. Rachel gives a quick glance behind her. She catches Fergus taking a quick sip from a hip flask which he hides again inside his jacket.

A moment between them.

As the music ends a man called HAYNES [forties] moves to the podium to give an appreciation of Frankie. The congregation is held spellbound. Haynes, an ex-officer, is handsome, charismatic and a brilliant communicator. He really means what he says and the congregation's mood is further heightened by the catch in his throat.

                    HAYNES
          Rachel asked for this beautiful music to be
          played… Not so much Verdi's 'Chorus of

Hebrew Slaves' as 'Frankie's Chorus of Expat
Contractors' [lots of grins and chuckles from
those with crew cuts]... by far the best party
piece in the Green Zone!... You all know what
an extrovert he was at times... and just like his
dress sense... [a few smiles]... you never knew
what to expect with Frankie... he always
broke the stereotype... He was recognised as a
terrific soldier... courageous, loyal, funny,
tough as nails... but always fair... ask the men
in uniform here today who had the deepest
respect for him... that doesn't come lightly,
believe me... it's earned under pressure... Well
let me tell you this... Frankie the man didn't
change when he left the army and came to
work for my company. He was still that same
decent human being. The skills he learned as a
soldier protected engineers bringing water and
electricity to the long-suffering civilians in
Baghdad. He protected surgeons, doctors,
electoral advisors, journalists and experts on
child nutrition. He believed in his work...
[looking up at the congregation] believed it
was worth risking his life for... [pause] Frankie
was a protector... a nation builder... a force
for good... it shames me to say this but there
are no monuments in this country to men like
Frankie... no Union Jacks nor guards of
honour... no sympathetic words from
politicians... in fact... little respect... even
worse... insults... called 'mercenaries'. Let me
never hear that word again. In my book they
are the great unsung heroes of our time...

Patriots... Warriors for peace. I want to say to
Rachel and family it was a privilege to have
spent time with this gentle giant and I am
proud to call him my friend. Rest in peace
Frankie...

Everyone is touched.

Fergus watches as Haynes takes his place behind Rachel. She turns to him and hugs him. Other emotional family members shake his hand in gratitude.

Fergus's face darkens and his agitation grows.

OUTSIDE THE CHURCH: The undertakers open up the back of the hearse in preparation for the coffin. The first mourners stream out, including two in wheelchairs.

INSIDE THE CHURCH: As the congregation leave Fergus is stunned to see a tall darker-skinned woman [thirties, attractive] on the last pew in the corner of the church. She is deeply upset. Fergus moves towards her. They clasp each other urgently.

Rachel, shocked, stops for a moment in the aisle to watch them. Both Fergus and the woman catch her look.

Fergus's face drops. He turns his back on Rachel.

Rachel leaves.

Craig, with his white stick, heads out too.

Fergus, and MARISOL, the dark-haired woman, with a recognisable Spanish accent, talk quietly as the last of the mourners leave. She tries to pull herself together.

MARISOL

He was desperate to speak to you... where
were you?

FERGUS

Been a bad boy Marisol... [She wants to know
more, and waits for an explanation] I went
with Craig to a night club... A pair of
bouncers wouldn't let him in... started taking
the piss about how he looked... I told them it
happened in Baghdad... one of them started
laughing at his white stick... we exchanged
opinions... they ended up in hospital... I
ended up in a police cell...

MARISOL

You are falling apart Fergus... you can't live
like this... Come back with me to Ibiza for a
while?... Calm down, no drink, no drugs...

Fergus stares at her gentle face.

FERGUS

I can't leave the country... they have taken
away my passport... I'll come after the court
case...

MARISOL

You promise?

Fergus nods.

Marisol takes a small brown package from her handbag and
hands it to Fergus.

MARISOL (CONT'D)

Jamie came to my bar on his way home from
Baghdad… gave me this… but it came from
Frankie who was still out there…

FERGUS

What is it?

MARISOL

No idea… I didn't open it… it had this little
note attached…

He reads it.

FERGUS

'Dearest Marisol… Keep this safe for me… or
give it to Fergus… Nobody else. Got to rush…
can't wait to see you, Love… Frankie'… Did
Jamie say what it was?

MARISOL

No.

Fergus looks at the package and then sticks it in his pocket. He
looks like a lost boy. She gives him a hug but he can hardly
respond.

4. HOTEL

Reception after the cremation.

A couple of hours have passed and lots of drink has been
consumed. By a bar several soldiers and contractors are in a
more rowdy mood.

Inside a private room off the bar Andrew Haynes, General
Manager, and ALEX WALKER, 'in country' Manager in Iraq,

[but joint owners of the company] give a straightforward account of how Frankie died to close members of his family: Rachel, Frankie's two brothers GARY and ANDY, his sister MICHELLE and heartbroken MOTHER.

Walker [with papers set down before him] sits alongside Haynes who in turn sits opposite the family.

Fergus has pulled up a chair between Rachel and Frankie's mother. He drinks from a pint of Guinness – far from his first of the day. He puts his hand over the mother's which is on the table.

> WALKER
> They were on Route Irish at the time of the attack…

Haynes spots their confusion.

> HAYNES
> Nickname for the road between Baghdad airport and the Green Zone… fortified area for the government and foreign contractors… called Route Irish because the Infantry Regiment, 'the fighting 69th', that patrolled there were traditionally recruited from Irish Americans…

He looks to Walker who continues again.

> WALKER
> …they were on their way to pick up a Spanish journalist from the airport…

> FERGUS
> His name?

Gary and Andy are annoyed by his tone and intervention. Walker checks his papers.

WALKER
Sergio Perez Minguez...

FERGUS
Which paper?

ANDY
Does it really matter?

WALKER
El País. [Pause] They were ambushed two kilometres from the airport by terrorists. No direct eye witnesses but [passing over copies to Rachel] I have signed statements by contractors from another company who passed by within minutes. They saw the car already in flames with the tyres shot out...

FERGUS
Soft-skinned or armoured?

WALKER
It was one from our new fleet just in from Kuwait... armoured...

FERGUS
Do you have a photograph?

More embarrassed glances between some of them.

HAYNES
I thought it might be too upsetting for the family on a day like this, Fergus... I'll have a copy sent to your home, Rachel, if you want?

She looks to the table and then nods.

WALKER

One of the contractors recognised Frankie
who was lying on the road outside the vehicle
and pulled to a halt...

FERGUS

What was his name and which company?

GARY

Let him finish for God's sake!

MOTHER

[Sharp] He can ask what he wants... he's
family as far as I am concerned...

HAYNES

It's all in the report Mrs Duncan...

WALKER

Frankie and two contractors were shot outside
the vehicle... we think they got out and
managed to return fire before they were
overrun... The driver's incinerated body was
still inside the car... the passing contractors still
rushed Frankie to hospital... Here is a signed
statement by the American doctor on duty...
autopsy report and death certificate...

FERGUS

Who were the other boys killed?

WALKER

Three Colombians...

HAYNES

Ex-soldiers… top professionals… the journalist
specially asked for some Spanish speakers…
I'm so sorry… Route Irish is the most
dangerous road in the world… they just
happened to be in the wrong place at the
wrong time…

Fergus jumps up suddenly.

FERGUS

Not Frankie!

The rest are stunned.

FERGUS (CONT'D)

He was never in the wrong place at the wrong
time!… [Looking down at the mother] He had
a thing about him… didn't he?… [To the
others] You don't understand… he was born
lucky…

Upset and embarrassment all round.

GARY

Fuck it! Get him out of here before I lose my
temper!

Fergus's eyes flash at them all. He walks out. Silence.

MICHELLE

I'm sorry…

MOTHER

[Again, sharp] Nothing to be sorry about…
those boys were like brothers from their first
day at school…

Rachel takes the mother's hand now.

                    GARY
          [Under his breath] Fucking nutter... that's
          what he is...

                    HAYNES
          ...Give him time... he's feeling guilty... and
          to be honest with you all there is some bad
          blood between us... Fergus worked with us,
          poached clients, broke his contract... and set
          up his own company. Stress and danger got to
          him... no shame in that... but he needs
          professional help and my company will gladly
          pay for it... maybe you can persuade him,
          Rachel, to see someone?

                    RACHEL
          I'll try...

                    HAYNES
          Does he ever see his family?

The mother and Rachel shake their heads.

                    MOTHER
          His mother up and left for London after she
          got remarried... any family life that boy had
          was with me and Frankie...

                    HAYNES
          He's a good man with a big heart... if you
          have any questions at all here's my card...
          phone me any time... day or night... I mean
          that.

ANDY

Thanks Andrew…

They all head towards the door. Rachel is last out. Walker takes
her by the arm.

WALKER

Rachel… do you want us to send Frankie's
personal effects to your home?

RACHEL

Yes… please do that…

WALKER

Just a small thing… Frankie borrowed a mobile
from one of our Iraqi drivers and never got a
chance to hand it back… worth nothing but
the driver had photographs of his son on it…
unfortunately his son was killed a week later…
for sentimental reasons he's desperate to get it
back… by any chance did Frankie mention it?

RACHEL

No… that's terrible… I'm so sorry…

WALKER

Don't worry about it… if it turns up
somewhere maybe you let me know…

RACHEL

Of course I will…

WALKER

Thanks Rachel… call me too if you need
anything. I'll be working in England for the
next month.

BY THE BAR – LATER: Fergus, another pint in hand, is in the middle of a rowdy bunch of men, some uniformed and others not, but it is apparent they are contractors by their cut. He's obviously very popular. Animated conversation between them all.

Suddenly Fergus notices Haynes in another corner talking to a fresh-faced young soldier in uniform. They are in polite conversation. Haynes hands the young soldier his business card.

FERGUS
Fuck... did you see that? What a wanker!

He charges over to Haynes, grabs him violently by the lapels and crashes him up against the wall with great force.

FERGUS (CONT'D)
Touting for business... at Frankie's funeral!

His mates rush over and try to restrain him.

YOUNG SOLDIER
I asked him for the card Fergus... calm down!

FERGUS
Money grabbing scumbag!

Fergus is ferocious and it takes several men some time to pull him off Haynes and get him to the ground. Still he writhes around on the ground like a man possessed.

Rachel rushes over.

RACHEL
This won't bring him back Fergus...

It stops him in his tracks. Several men still hold him down.

RACHEL (CONT'D)
It's not his fault.

Fergus, breathing heavily, seems to calm. She lays a hand on his arm.

RACHEL (CONT'D)
Let him go…

Haynes, ever the gentleman, quietly backs off without making any more fuss and disappears from the room.

5. FERGUS'S FLAT, BY DOCKS, LIVERPOOL – EVENING

Fergus, still wearing the same clothes as for the funeral [with a ripped sleeve hanging off his jacket], uncorks another bottle of wine in his luxury flat down by the Albert docks. It is the type of expensive place a young footballer might have. But the place is virtually empty; almost antiseptic.

Fergus pulls the package he received from Marisol from his pocket. He pulls off the covering to reveal a scuffed mobile phone. He examines it and tries to switch it on. Dead. He examines the packaging carefully to make sure there is no hidden note. Nothing. Fergus tries his charger. The telephone comes to life but it only has Arabic script he can't understand.

He stares at it for a moment before leaving it on the bench charging.

Fergus doesn't bother with a glass. He grips the bottle of wine and walks over to the answering machine. He clicks it on. [We hear some of the same messages from before.]

As Frankie's voice booms out Fergus makes his way over to the sliding door and balcony. He stares out over the old docks towards the Liver building and the River Mersey beyond. In the distance he can still hear Frankie's voice.

VOICE OFF

Hey... Cuntylugs! Frankie here...Where are you? Give me a call. [Click] Hey Dick Head... did you get my message on your mobile?... Phone me back... this is an order! [Click] Fergus... Come on man... I'm getting tired of this... midnight your time... phone me when you get in... doesn't matter how late... I'll still be up counting the stars... got to speak mate. [Click. Another, now much more serious.] Fergus... Are you on the piss again? I really need to speak to you... phone me... [Click. Now urgent] Fergus... [pause]... Fuck! I need you man! I need you now! Not tomorrow... Now! Fucking phone me! I'm all mixed up... [deep frustration] Just piss off!... useless fucking waster... [pause, resigned]... Phone me when you can Fergus... I'm up against it here... [struggling and sense of panic] I don't know what to do man... I really don't know what to fucking do... need your help mate... I need you... I need you Fergus...

As Fergus stares his mind drifts back and he smiles...

FRANKIE'S VOICE

[Dynamic comic tone]... House was a shithole... fucking freezing man... bare floor... baby screaming and this cross-eyed geriatric granda stuck in the corner...

6. OLD BAR, LIVERPOOL – THREE YEARS AGO

Fergus and Frankie, both wearing Liverpool football colours, are standing at a bar having a drink. Frankie, big, tough and comic, is in full flight telling a story as Fergus is nearly doubled up sick with laughter.

FRANKIE
...Never moved an inch, thought he'd been stuffed!... I handed over the court order... non-payment of a gas bill... the missus went ballistic, started waving a chopper at me... cursing like a banshee... she opens the kitchen door and sets this fucking wolf on me... picked up a chair to defend myself... the old fucker came to life... clapping his hands and laughing like a maniac... 'Go on Spot... rip his balls off!'

Fergus is laughing his head off.

FERGUS
What did you do?

FRANKIE
Ran like fuck!... Flying down the stairs with that monster cunt snapping at me... terrified... beast jumped up and caught me by the arse!

FERGUS
You're joking...

Frankie has a quick squint round the bar and drops his tracksuit trousers to reveal a bruised arse and an angry wound.

FRANKIE

Five fucking stitches and half my arse gone...
lucky still to have me hole... probably die a
slow death foaming at the mouth... Christ... I
was safer in the army... fucking sick of it
man...

More hilarity from Fergus.

FERGUS

Better be paying you well...

FRANKIE

That's a joke... a fucking bailiff...

A moment between them.

FERGUS

Why don't you come with me to Iraq? Join the
circuit.

Frankie shakes his head.

FRANKIE

Rachel would go crazy... I promised her I'd
stay in Civvy Street... no way back now...

FERGUS

Does she still dream about her own private
gym?

FRANKIE

Studio. Heart set on it! Both of us... we're
saving every penny...

FERGUS

I'm getting paid ten grand a month... a
glorified bodyguard... won't get this chance
ever again.

It takes a moment to register.

FRANKIE

Fuck...

FERGUS

Tax free. Can get you a job right now... one
phone call... on my team.

Frankie stares at him.

FERGUS (CONT'D)

Ask her... [pause] Tell her.

FERGUS'S FLAT – BALCONY:

Fergus takes another long swig from the bottle.

6A. AIRPORT (FLASHBACK)

Departures. Fergus waits at the security checkpoint. As Frankie
and Rachel embrace some yards away he catches a glimpse of
them between passengers. Frankie's big frame engulfs her as she
leans her head on his chest. Frankie wipes a tear from her
cheek as they hold each other's eye.

FRANKIE

You know I love you to pieces...

RACHEL

Me too...

FRANKIE

I'll be safer out there… no big dogs biting my
arse in Walton and buckets of shite from top
windows…

She smiles between her tears. They grip each other again for
one last long embrace.

They split.

They wave to each other as Frankie drifts into the queue.
Fergus, further ahead, catches a glimpse of her wave one last
time.

FERGUS'S FLAT – BALCONY:

Fergus pulls deeply on a cigarette as he looks out over the
Mersey and distant lights on the far shore.

7. BAGHDAD (FLASHBACK) – EIGHTEEN MONTHS AGO

Vehicles 1 and 2 manned by contractors rattle along a dusty
road. The first is a typical overt PSD Counter Assault Truck. [It
looks like a heavy 4x4 apart from home-made armour at the
back, with a machine gun sticking out over the top.] It
contains three contractors. The second is a Toyota Surf 4x4.

Fergus and Frankie sit in the back seats of the second vehicle
with 'a package' [a client] between them. They are both armed
to the teeth but wear sandy-coloured clothes favoured by
contractors and not army uniform. Down between their legs
they grip short-barrelled M4 carbines. A 'commentary' [a run-
down of dangers they confront as they drive along] can be
heard from the contractor in the front seat in the first vehicle
via a fist mike each contractor has.

CONTRACTOR

Abandoned truck... left... 50 metres... group
of kids... right... man carrying package... left
40 metres... traffic merging right... 75
metres... dead animal left... 30 metres...
bridge straight head... 40 metres... bridge all
clear...

Frankie, back right, notices two bodies pop up over the lip of a
building.

FRANKIE

[Shouting into his fist mike] Ambush right!
On the roof!

Just as Frankie opens fire through his own windscreen the
vehicle is rocked by an RPG grenade which destroys the
engine. The front side of the vehicle is sprayed by gunfire but
bounces off the armoured Kevlar plates. As the vehicle skids to
a halt Frankie continues to fire [repeated single shot] at the
men on the roof to keep them pinned down.

On the ambush side in and amongst the buildings some seventy
yards away; one insurgent has the RPG, another has a heavier
machine gun, and three have AK47s. Fergus grabs the terrified
client and pulls him out from his door [back left], and pushes
him down to the ground behind the vehicle. The two
contractors in the front seat scramble out of the protected side
and return fire too.

Fergus now leans over the bonnet of the vehicle and covers
Frankie who scrambles from the Toyota.

FERGUS

[Firing] Move it Frankie!

The first vehicle – positioned some thirty-five yards ahead, is now returning fire too from the heavier machine gun positioned at the back door. There is the merest glimpse of four insurgent figures disappearing in the distance between buildings and then silence.

The shooting stops.

Fergus, Frankie and the other contractors scan the horizon. When he judges it to be safe Frankie [accompanied by the two contractors from the front seat of the second vehicle], grabs the shaken client from the ground. They shield him with their bodies as they rush him to the safety of the first vehicle while Fergus stays behind to provide cover.

After the client is bundled into the safety of vehicle 1 Frankie beckons Fergus. As Fergus now sprints from burning vehicle 2 to vehicle 1 Frankie notices a body pop up from another roof [the inexperienced insurgent is 'skylighted'] to shoot Fergus.

Frankie expertly picks him off. The body flies back with the impact. Fergus scrambles in beside Frankie.

                    FERGUS (CONT'D)
          Frankie boy… thanks man…

7A. FERGUS'S FLAT – DAY

Fergus lies back on a camp bed in the corner of his enormous sitting room. Verdi's 'Chorus of Hebrew Slaves', blasting out at top volume, builds to a chorus as Fergus stares into space…

8. SECURITY QUARTERS – BAGHDAD

The very same chorus builds to a crescendo, as Frankie, bare chested, directs like an extroverted conductor. [Rachel's name is tattooed round his powerful bicep.]

Before him is his imaginary Hebrew chorus – a dozen or so security guards [most are recognisable from the ambush, including Fergus who really enjoys Frankie's antics], well-oiled, crashing back on settees, holding cold beers too, who join in 'Da da da' style without the words, to the music blasting out on powerful speakers.

They are killing themselves at Frankie's hammed up conductor performance... now the crescendo and fists are punched in the air like football supporters.

FRANKIE
[Shouting out] Whistle Yi Fuckin Expat Slaves!

ALL TOGETHER
[Response] And that's an order!

Led by Frankie, and trying not to laugh, the dozen men now 'whistle' the chorus. They really let off steam after danger; closest of friends, arms round shoulders, physical contact, and much hilarity at Frankie's big daft concentrated whistling face.

FERGUS'S SITTING ROOM:

Fergus sits in exactly the same position. Total silence. He stares at the wall.

9. STREET AND RACHEL'S FLAT

Fergus, dressed in a tracksuit, runs at speed by a lovely old Georgian terrace. He sprints now along by a beautifully laid-out square. He stops and checks his time. He approaches one of the pristine entrances and presses a doorbell.

RACHEL'S FLAT:

The sitting room is a jumbled mess of miscellaneous material belonging to Frankie.

Fergus, still dressed in the tracksuit, drinks a cup of tea. Rachel is trying to sort out Frankie's shoes, clothes, boxes, and miscellaneous files. She looks overwhelmed and confused.

Fergus, sipping from his cup, examines a couple of tastefully framed photographs of Frankie and Rachel together which are placed on the mantelpiece. [There is one of them on the top of a mountain together. Rachel balances precariously, laughing, on top of his shoulders. In another, both of them have shaken up a bottle of champagne and spray it towards the unseen onlookers as they celebrate the opening of their studio. Both look elated. There is another simple one of Frankie snoozing against a tree with a map over his lap.]

Rachel picks up a pair of shoes and then a huge overcoat.

> RACHEL
> He was that big... don't know if they'll fit
> anybody else...

She picks up a shirt. She holds it to her face and takes a deep breath.

> RACHEL (CONT'D)
> I can still smell him...

She picks up another and does the same. Fergus doesn't know what to do and they hold eyes for a moment. She indicates a trunk.

RACHEL (CONT'D)
His stuff from Iraq arrived this morning...
[pause, picking up a framed photograph and
CD of Verdi] I found these wrapped up in a
towel on the very top and couldn't go on...

She hands Fergus a framed photograph of her and Frankie walking through the finishing line of a half marathon together, hand in hand. She has a bandage round her knee. They are looking at each other – like early lovers.

RACHEL (CONT'D)
[Examining the photo] The week after you
introduced us... half marathon... my knee was
playing up but I wanted to finish... he walked
the last three miles with me... he took my
hand for the first time as we crossed the line...

FERGUS
He had that on the wall above his bunk.

It gets her.

RACHEL
I gave him a lift home after the run... my
radio was tuned to Classic FM... joked we
could never have anything in common... by
chance 'Chorus of Hebrew Slaves' came on...
halfway through I caught him looking at me...
I blushed so much... that was it.

FERGUS

So that's where he got it from… drove us all
round the fucking bend with that.

She chuckles and then takes refuge in a little box of
photographs. She flicks through them. There are photographs
of Fergus and Frankie as contractors in Iraq. There is a
disturbing one of a car in flames and incinerated bodies inside,
and another of a burnt out truck and considerable bunker.
There are several of Fergus alone – oiling his weapons, in a
market place, or sitting on the back of a truck with his
weapon.

RACHEL

Here's a surprise… another one of you…

Fergus, embarrassed, glances at a comic one, domestic, close-up
of a smiling Fergus brushing his teeth.

RACHEL (CONT'D)

I never looked at these before… we had an
unwritten rule… he never talked about it… I
never asked… I used to pretend you were both
in Belize again… in the Caribbean and not
the desert… if it came on the TV I turned it
off… if someone asked I'd change the subject
and they never asked again… once I caught a
glimpse of that poor man in the orange
jumpsuit… I nearly fainted Fergus… I built a
complete barrier in my mind… I never asked
him once how it was… not once Fergus… can
you believe that?!

She lifts another of his shirts to her face and breathes deeply.

RACHEL (CONT'D)
But I took his money… didn't I?

FERGUS
Don't Rachel…

RACHEL
I've got my studio… my trendy little yellow
Mini…

She picks up a little container.

RACHEL (CONT'D)
…and now I've got his ashes.

FERGUS
Don't punish yourself like this… he loved you
so much Rachel…

She grips on to them for a moment as she tries to control
herself and then lays them down again. Fergus stares at the
container.

RACHEL
I don't know what to do with them…

Fergus hesitates for a long moment.

FERGUS
Do you want me to take them for you?

She stares at him for a moment in disbelief.

RACHEL
What did you say?

He looks away and stares at his hands.

RACHEL (CONT'D)

He's fucking dead and you're still clinging
on!... You had so much of him... more than
me... You had enough!

FERGUS

I'm sorry Rachel... I thought you wouldn't
mind...

RACHEL

Wouldn't mind!... You took him to Iraq! If it
wasn't for you he'd never have gone... even
now you want to take him from me...
sometimes... [pause] I hate you Fergus!

FERGUS

I better go...

RACHEL

Who was the woman at the back of the
church? [Silence] Who was she?

FERGUS

She's from Ibiza. [Her expression demands
explanation] A lot of the single boys used to
stop off there before coming home... a way of
'coming down'... every day could be your last
out there... hard to come from that to
shopping in Tesco's...

RACHEL

What was her name?

FERGUS

Marisol... she ran a little bar we liked... she
was patient with us... once she knew...

RACHEL

Friend or girlfriend?

Fergus looks at her.

FERGUS

Does it matter Rachel?... A little bit of both...

RACHEL

What about Frankie?

FERGUS

No! He never came... he never knew her.

She stares through him.

RACHEL

She came all that way for you?... [pause] I saw
her during the service... she wasn't crying...
she was sobbing... I always picked you up
together at the airport... [dawning on her]...
Frankie was with you too...

Fergus's head goes down.

FERGUS

You don't understand Rachel... it was a safe
place in no man's land before coming home...
just crazy time with mates without being
terrified of getting your balls blown off...

RACHEL

Fucking time.

FERGUS

Just trying to clear all that shit out of our
heads... his real flesh-and-blood life was back
here with you!

RACHEL

You shared her…

He can't hold her eye.

RACHEL (CONT'D)

You two shared everything! Look at me! You owe me that!

Fergus looks up at last.

FERGUS

Yeah… we shared everything… apart from you.

She whacks him across the face.

FERGUS (CONT'D)

You'll have to do it much harder than that.

She does. Much harder.

FERGUS (CONT'D)

Harder Rachel.

They hold each other's eye. She's stunned by what she has done.

10. OUTSIDE AND INTO REFUGEE CENTRE, LIVERPOOL

Fergus walks by a dozen or so foreign men and women who are waiting outside the refugee centre and into the reception.

FERGUS

I have an appointment with Harim… [brief hesitation from receptionist]… the Iraqi musician…

The receptionist nods and picks up the phone.

PRIVATE ROOM:

Fergus sits with HARIM. [He speaks good English, has charisma and a dark sense of humour.] The mobile phone from Frankie is connected by wires to a TV set so that the images recorded on the phone are a respectable size.

Harim skilfully handles his way through the Arabic text. He finds several photographs. Domestic scenes. A middle-aged mother is cooking something, and she stands by what looks like her two sons, around late teens or early twenties.

Another. She holds up a dish and she is laughing as one of the sons clowns around her. Harim smiles.

> HARIM
> [Pronouncing the food in Arabic]...
> Delicious... makes me homesick... [more
> fiddling with mobile]... there's a video clip...
> do you want to see them?

Fergus nods. Harim clicks. It is obviously a birthday party. Again Harim smiles at the familiar scene.

Without warning the party is cut and the screen fills with something much more dramatic, and more familiar to Fergus. He leans forward as the camera focuses in on the back of a typical overt PSD [Personal Security Detail] − like a 4x4 − with spare tyre, and rear gunner − the barrel sticks out of the back of the vehicle above home-made armour. There is also a notice in Arabic script and English warning everyone to keep their distance.

There are shouts, punctuated by gunfire, recorded on the mobile between Iraqi voices which Harim translates as simultaneously as possible; they are shocked, angry and under great stress. On screen Fergus and Harim can see a figure shoot from the back of the PSD.

> HARIM (CONT'D)
> [Translating the shouts]... The dog's shooting!
> Shit... he's hit the taxi! [Like an argument
> between two men] Yosuf! Out of here now!...
> Wait a minute... I've got to get this... get
> closer... just a second... I want out of here
> now! Two seconds...

The camera moves closer to the taxi which has skidded to a stop. Obviously someone is now running to the taxi as he holds the phone to record... there is a glimpse of chaos and bloodshed inside. The taxi driver and passengers have been killed or wounded. Both figures in the front look dead, while an adolescent in the back, with a chest wound, moaning, looks like he's dying. A woman, covered in blood, beside him looks dead too.

> HARIM (CONT'D)
> [Translating] Bastards! They've killed a
> family... what can we do?... [sudden panic]
> They've stopped the Jeep!... Get back on the
> bike Yosuf!... Back on the fucking bike... one
> of them is coming and he's got a gun!

It looks like the boy holding the phone has ducked down behind the bonnet of a car caught up in the chaos. The camera catches sight of a contractor, holding his rifle, running back towards the taxi. Fergus is stunned as he recognises Frankie.

Frankie stares in horror at the bloodbath inside the taxi.

                            FRANKIE

Fuck Nelson! You slotted a whole fucking
family arsehole!

                             VOICE

[From Jeep] Frankie! Get back in the fucking
Jeep now!

Frankie opens the taxi door and the dead driver tumbles out.

                            FRANKIE

Oh fuck...

                             VOICE

I'll fucking leave you if you don't get back!

The camera catches the two Westerners in a wild slanging
match without getting many of the words but the body
language is clear; they are furious with each other.

Suddenly the man at the back of the Jeep has noticed the figure
with the mobile phone crouching behind the car. He raises his
voice and points in the direction of the phone/camera.

More panicked shouts in Arabic.

                            HARIM

He's seen you! Back on the bike Yosuf... now!

The gun is raised in the camera's direction. Now a blur as the
figure presumably runs for his life.

                       HARIM (CONT'D)

Run!... Faster Yosuf!

They hear a bike revving up and a faster blur on the screen;
sounds now of gunfire and terrible screaming as the mobile
crashes to the ground.

Now all blue on screen as it films the sky. More terrible screams...

HARIM (CONT'D)
[Moaning] Yosuf... I can't move... Yosuf...

More machine-gun fire. Silence.

FRANKIE'S VOICE
Stop... fucking moron!

VOICE
Back in the Jeep you stupid cunt... Back here!

FRANKIE'S VOICE
Jesus Christ... they're just lads...

A hand darkens the screen and it all goes blank. Fergus is stunned. Harim is solemn. They both stare at the blank screen for some long moments. Fergus tries to hide his shock.

HARIM
Do you know these men?

Fergus shakes his head.

HARIM (CONT'D)
Have you ever been to Iraq?

FERGUS
No.

Harim stares at him. He can feel his blood boil.

HARIM
Murdering cowards!... Bulletproof vests...
armoured trucks... machine guns! Shoot who
they want! Have you heard of Order 17?

Fergus's eyes drop to the table.

HARIM (CONT'D)

Order 17 was forced upon us by the
Americans... gives these mercenaries freedom
to act like cowboys... total immunity! They
cannot be touched by Iraqi law... they charge
through our country killing who they want,
when they want... no questions asked... all
they care about is money... we detest them
even more than the army... [Pointing at the
screen] This is murder. Who are you?

FERGUS

I told you... I am a freelance researcher
working for an investigative journalist... will
you help us?

HARIM

That depends. Where did you get this?

FERGUS

I'm sorry... it's confidential... I want to find
out exactly what happened... who owned this
phone... anything about him... can you go
through it... texts... messages... names...
phone numbers... translate everything for
me... there might even be another witness out
there somewhere...

Harim stares at him, trying to figure him out.

FERGUS (CONT'D)

I'll pay you well... seven hundred pounds to
account.

The amount surprises – and impresses – him. Fergus hands over a thick envelope with cash in it.

> HARIM
> What's to stop me copying this and putting it
> on the net?

> FERGUS
> If you do that you will jeopardise the whole
> investigation... the contractors will close ranks,
> falsify records and have the men prepared with
> the best lawyers in the country... we won't
> find out a thing... At present they don't even
> know it exists... I want to interview them one
> by one... unguarded...

Harim continues to stare. He picks up the phone again and examines it.

> FERGUS (CONT'D)
> Do I have your word you won't copy this...
> and keep it confidential?

> HARIM
> They kill people all the time... why are you
> interested in this case?

Fergus hesitates.

> FERGUS
> The contractor who ran to the taxi... he died
> ten days ago... I think the company who
> employed him are lying... hiding something...

> HARIM
> Ah... that's why you care... What about the
> Iraqis? Do they count?

Again Harim holds his eye.

                    FERGUS
          I just want to know the truth…

                    HARIM
          The truth… in Iraq?

Another moment between them.

                    FERGUS
          Does the video have a date?

Harim checks.

                    HARIM
          1st of September 2007.

                    FERGUS
          Four weeks ago.

                    HARIM
          Why should I trust you?

                    FERGUS
          You shouldn't trust anybody.

Harim stares at him for a moment and then nods.

                    HARIM
          Okay.

He picks up the money.

11. FOOTBALL PITCH – LIVERPOOL

Fergus watches Craig play blind football. Craig charges around
like a mad man as he chases the sound of bells attached to the
ball. As Craig runs by Fergus shouts at him.

FERGUS

Behind you ya daft prick!

CRAIG

Fuck off!

Craig collides with a much smaller player and sends him flying.
Fergus bursts out laughing.

FERGUS

Are you fucking blind as well Ref? Red card!

Craig turns in his direction, smiling openly and gives Fergus
the finger, unperturbed by his lack of good taste.

LATER: Fergus and Craig sit on a bench by the field having a
drink.

CRAIG

He phoned about three fucking times looking
for you...

FERGUS

Did he mention Nelson?

CRAIG

Gave him a mouthful... and those two wankers
at the funeral too...

FERGUS

Haynes and Walker?

CRAIG

Cursed them to hell and back but didn't make
much sense... he wanted you... When I told
him you were on the piss he went nuts... didn't
sound like Frankie...

FERGUS

Can you remember the date?

CRAIG

Not long after you flattened the bouncers...

FERGUS

Could it have been the 1st of September?

CRAIG

Was that a Saturday?

FERGUS

Yeah... Saturday.

CRAIG

Must have been... right after our game. What's
going on?

12. FERGUS'S FLAT

A room in Fergus's flat, empty apart from one simple desk, a
computer and one seat.

Fergus is on Skype [telephone conversation via computer but
with images of each speaker on screen, slightly out of sync]
with his mate TOMMY who is in Baghdad.

Fergus, sharp, focussed and with the notebook beside him to
which he refers now and again, goes through his list of
questions which he ticks off with a pencil. It is obvious that he
has done his homework before calling.

Tommy, on screen, looks increasingly uncomfortable as the
conversation continues.

TOMMY

Why can't you come out here yourself?
Fuck!... Could be blacklisted...

FERGUS

I will, after the court case... Fuck it Tommy!
You're in and out of the office all the time...
get me a copy of the incident report... 1st
September... shooting on the taxi... if there
are handwritten notes scan them... send them
over...

TOMMY

If I get caught they'll go nuts man...

FERGUS

[Checking his notebook] Who else was in the
vehicle with Frankie and Nelson?... names and
numbers... Frankie was really upset that
night... Ask Peggy at the bar if she knows
anything... they were close... and I've got to
find Jamie...

TOMMY

Jock mechanic?... He's fucked off to
Afghanistan...

FERGUS

See if anyone can get a number for him... it's
really important...

TOMMY

Jesus Christ...

FERGUS

I need to know who died alongside Frankie on

the 17th of September. Names and contact numbers. [Ticking off more points on his list] Any rumours... loose talk around the bars... ask Ralph... he's a nosey bastard and knows all the scandal... This is a long shot... but there must have been some Iraqi witnesses...

TOMMY

[Stunned] Fuck Fergus! How in the name of Christ can I do that?

FERGUS

Ask my old driver... Hasim... he's ex-cop and still has family in the Iraqi police... tell him I'll pay him well if he can find a witness... a big fucking bonus... that's a promise...

TOMMY

The cunt will just make it up...

FERGUS

Is Nelson out there?

TOMMY

Saw him last night... mouthing off as usual.

FERGUS

I need to know when he's coming home.

Tommy just stares for a few moments.

TOMMY

I'm not messing around with him...

FERGUS

Tommy... this is really important... I need to
know where he was on the 17th of
September... the day Frankie died...

Tommy is shaking his head on the screen.

TOMMY

Fuck man... if he gets wind I'm asking
questions... no way!... You know what he's
like...

FERGUS

Well just check the rota... see if he was on
duty, off duty... in Baghdad or in the
provinces... that's all I'm asking...

Tommy is shaking his head on screen again.

TOMMY

I'm not messing with Nelson... I've got three
kids to look after... [squirming on screen]
Fuck! I could lose my job Fergus...

FERGUS

We owe Frankie... both of us.

13. FERGUS'S BALCONY – LATER

Fergus stands on an enormous balcony looking out over the
Mersey. He has a pair of binoculars in his hands. He focuses in
on the ferry halfway across the Mersey heading for the other
side.

Way below he's amazed to see a yellow Mini pull up outside.
He looks down as Rachel gets out of the car. She stops and
stares up.

INSIDE FLAT:

Rachel examines the almost empty flat as Fergus prepares a cup of tea in an enormous kitchen-come-sitting-room. She peeks in at an empty bedroom, and then another. The study has one desk and computer. She can't help but notice a little camp bed – perfectly tidy, military style, with blanket folded tight, up against the wall in the sitting room. She is impressed by the stunning view.

RACHEL

> You kept this quiet... how long have you had
> the place?

FERGUS

> Months... lost track.

RACHEL

> And still empty... what's going on Fergus?

FERGUS

> Didn't know where to start...

She smiles.

RACHEL

> So you curl up in a corner?

Fergus smiles to himself as he looks round the huge empty space.

FERGUS

> Fucking stupid idea... half the time I go round
> to Craig's and sleep on his sofa...

It gets her. He hands her a cup.

                              RACHEL
            I'm sorry for what I said to you...

                              FERGUS
            You were right... if it wasn't for me...

She cuts him off sharply.

                              RACHEL
            Shhhhh...

Silence between them for a moment. She takes a little box from
her pocket and hands it to him. Fergus hesitates, then opens it.
He lifts up a tasteful little pendant with a coloured stone surface
on a gold chain. Fergus looks at her.

                        RACHEL (CONT'D)
            It's what you want... some of Frankie's ashes...

Fergus is stunned. He struggles to hold himself together.

                        RACHEL (CONT'D)
            It's only right... if he wasn't with you, he
            talked about you... sometimes I felt I was in
            bed with the pair of you...

Fergus grips it tight.

                              FERGUS
            [Whispered] Thank you Rachel...

He chokes up and moves quickly to the toilet but the door is
not fully closed. Rachel can hear him splash water on his face
as he tries to pull himself together.

She follows him, leans up against the wall outside and then
slides down to sit on the floor, back to the wall.

RACHEL

I have to be honest... I was jealous. Know
what hurt me most? He didn't go to Iraq for
the money... he went to be with you...

FERGUS (VOICE OFF)

That's rubbish!

RACHEL

I think he loved you...

FERGUS (VOICE OFF)

Fuck off...

RACHEL

Loved you more than me...

FERGUS (VOICE OFF)

Cut it out Rachel.

RACHEL

Looking at all those pictures... I realised I
never really knew him...

FERGUS (VOICE OFF)

No Rachel... you just knew a different part of
him... the best part... without a gun in his
hand...

RACHEL

I bet Marisol knew him better... I bet she
asked questions...

Fergus comes out of the loo. His eyes are red. He sinks to his
backside too, his back leaning on the opposite wall. They stare
across at each other, feet almost touching. She can see the
pendant round his neck.

FERGUS

We got drunk... danced... [slight hesitation to
find the word]... messed around... tried to
forget... You were in a different league...
you've got to understand that... [passionate]...
he wanted to share his life with you... his eyes
fucking shone when he spoke about you... he
was only like that with you...

She stares at him.

FERGUS (CONT'D)
[Holding her eye] I'll never lie to you again.

She flicks her foot against his in appreciation.

RACHEL
I went through his trunk today... stuff from
Iraq.

FERGUS
Did you find his mobile... any messages?

RACHEL
A few... nothing important.

FERGUS
What about his laptop?

RACHEL
Must have got a bang... rattled as I picked it
up.

FERGUS
Did you check his email?

RACHEL

I don't know his password… [She can tell by
his expression] You do… don't you?… [Still he
hesitates] Scared I might find a few love notes
from Marisol?… Are you going to tell me?

There is a pause as he thinks.

FERGUS

Six letters…

Fergus pulls up his sleeve and reveals a tattoo round his upper
arm. Rachel's face colours in embarrassment. She's stunned.
She reads six letters…

FERGUS (CONT'D)

'Rachel'… that's his password.

She stares at him for a second, confused.

RACHEL

Same tattoo as Frankie's… same arm…

It's too intimate and too close for comfort. She can feel anger
mount.

RACHEL (CONT'D)

What is it with you two?!

FERGUS

We were really drunk… got it done
together… daft… I just copied him… he said
he loved you… I said… [pause, eye contact] I
met you first… and he burst out laughing…

Rachel suddenly kicks him a hard one.

RACHEL

Really stupid idea... [pause] What's your
password?

Fergus just looks at her.

RACHEL (CONT'D)

For Christ's sake... you're like fucking clones!
Who said you could use my name like that?

She looks away for several long moments as she wrestles with
the contradictions. Fergus continues to watch her.

FERGUS

They're hiding something Rachel...

RACHEL

[Sharp] I phoned the contractor who found
Frankie to thank him... I emailed the doctor
too... I emailed the Spanish journalist he was
going to pick up... Haynes gave me their
details like that... [snapping her fingers]... it
all ties up... Does that sound like a man who's
trying to hide something?

FERGUS

Can you remember if Frankie phoned you on
the 1st of September?

Rachel is surprised.

RACHEL

Dad's birthday... short call... we were eating
in a restaurant... he was really emotional...
[pause, self-conscious] said he loved me so
much and just wanted to get home... I was
over the moon and I celebrated with Dad...
Why?

FERGUS

Can I have the statements you got from
Haynes... [She nods] Did he send you the
photo of the burnt out vehicle?...

RACHEL

Not yet... but I got this from the contractor
who found him... their car on Route Irish.

She looks upset as she pulls out a photograph from her handbag
printed from her computer.

Fergus leans over and takes it.

He feels it in his gut as he studies the burning car. Flames and
smoke smother most of the wreckage although the shocking
burnt figure of the driver is still visible in the driver's seat.

RACHEL (CONT'D)

I can't bear thinking about it...

She is overcome. Fergus holds his head in his hands.

14. BY OLD DOCKLAND, LIVERPOOL

Fergus, in an expensive Audi sports, drives down by the
abandoned dock area. He approaches a run-down looking
street and steps out to a double lock-up.

He enters and turns on the light. It is full of miscellaneous stuff,
boxes in storage, and mostly exercise equipment, benches,
weights etc. He unlocks a heavy metal locker which has double
padlocks. He strips off to reveal a powerful build and puts on
his tracksuit.

He checks a drawer inside the locker. He picks up a stocky
hand gun, a Swiss-made Sigg P226, and a chunky box of

ammunition. Behind that is a knife, and several pairs of plastic cuffs. Right at the back there is an impressive long-barrelled rifle with telescopic sights attached [a black-coloured hunting rifle] which he handles carefully for a second.

He moves to a running machine and he sets it at a slow pace; begins to jog gently, his face in total concentration – the only sound now is of running feet.

Fergus fingers the pendant with Frankie's ashes which dangles and bounces as he runs.

> FERGUS'S VOICE
> I'm going to find out Frankie boy... I'm
> going to find out what happened... I give you
> my word Frankie... my word. You would do it
> for me... I'll do it for you... just like we
> promised...

He adjusts the running machine with a flick of his finger and the pace builds. The steady exercise, and sound of pounding feet, lead him to a dreamlike state.

Real images of the war in Iraq flash through his mind. [Not necessarily his, but incidents he has seen on the news or net, but which reflect his own experience.] Some of the following:

A brute sergeant soldier bawling obscenities at his own soldiers before battle.

Soldiers howling with laughter as they obliterate buildings with rockets.

Real targets, men, spotted by sophisticated night weapons – they appear like digital cartoon figures, who are then blown up like a video game.

LOCK-UP: Fergus is now running faster.

Sweeping jets, helicopter gunships, bombing of Fallujah, burnt out buildings that look like hell on earth.

Civilians screaming – some mutilated by white phosphorus.

Injured soldiers screaming. Young squaddies under terrible stress. Dead bodies. Some are weeping for a colleague.

Iraqi civilians, with hatred and fury, screaming at soldiers.

LOCK-UP: Fergus's running machine is at full pelt. His face streams with sweat as he fights for breath. As if he is punishing himself.

FLASHBACK (IRAQ):

A night raid in a humble house in Baghdad.

Fergus plus three other men from the SAS have already burst inside the front door. They are in full combat gear, and they have torches attached to their guns.

Fergus and Soldier 1 are inside a narrow sitting room. They stack up for a moment outside a bedroom door before charging in, while another two soldiers behind provide back-up.

As Fergus barges into the bedroom there are screams of terror from those sleeping inside. [A mother in her mid-thirties, a girl aged eleven, a boy aged nine, a youth aged seventeen, and a grandmother.]

Fergus's torch lights up the terrified faces as he bawls instructions at them to 'get down' in simple Arabic. He quickly realises there is no armed resistance, and that there is only one grown male, the youth aged seventeen.

One of the soldiers behind switches on a fluorescent light.

Fergus's gun swings on its strap as he grabs plastic cuffs to arrest the adolescent, but the very determined mother leaps in front of Fergus and refuses to move despite Fergus's instructions.

Fergus tries to push her away as she protects her petrified son in the corner and continues to shout vicious abuse at Fergus. Fergus pushes harder but the woman clings on to her son and fights back. The soldiers behind shout at Fergus to 'move it'.

Still the woman won't budge.

                    FERGUS
          Get out of here you stupid cow!

Still she battles, screaming all the while.

                    WOMAN
          [In Arabic] He's not done anything wrong...
          you took my husband too... I haven't seen him
          in four months... You're not taking my son
          too... he's only seventeen... get out of our
          country.

More impatient shouts from the soldiers outside which increases the pressure on Fergus.

                    SOLDIER 1
          Whack her one for Christ's sake!

The mother is now more hysterical than ever. Fergus bawls at her again. She grabs the barrel of his gun. Fergus snaps and punches her full on the face, knocking her out. The terrified adolescent is now screaming insults at him. Fergus completely loses it and starts punching and kicking the boy who drops to the ground and curls up in a ball to protect himself from Fergus's blows.

                    FERGUS
         Get up you dumb fucking Rag Head or I'll
         blow your brains out!

LOCK-UP: Fergus pounds on.

An orange jump-suited contractor [face blanked out] shakes in terror as fundamentalists pose behind him. A masked figure pulls out a sharpened knife and grabs the victim by the hair...

LOCK-UP: Fergus pushes to his agonising limit.

15. LIVERPOOL PUB – LATE

Fergus and Rachel are side by side in a quiet corner of an old pub.

There is an intimate and confessional tone between them.

                    FERGUS
         When I was in the SAS we did joint operations
         with US Special Forces... on the hunt for
         'terrorists'... most of them were just chicken
         farmers... doors blown off hinges... hooded...
         hands behind their backs... cuffs, wrists
         swelling up like balloons... pissing
         themselves... shitting themselves, children
         screaming... One night we did eleven houses
         in a row! If they didn't support Al Qaeda
         before they did after... [pause] Some were
         tortured by the Yanks...

RACHEL

How do you know?

FERGUS

I once saw them interrogating this guy we
picked up... they used an electric prod on him
first and then half drowned him in a swimming
pool...

Silence for a moment.

RACHEL

Did you say anything?

Fergus looks at his hands.

FERGUS

They used to bring them up to a place called
Camp Nama... we all knew what happened up
there... they had a motto, 'No blood, no foul.'

Rachel is shocked.

RACHEL

Leave no marks... was that it?

Fergus nods as he takes another sip from his drink.

FERGUS

I didn't sign up for that... I signed up to kill.

Rachel stares at him. She sees he means it.

RACHEL

Is that when you left?

FERGUS

One day I was attached to an American
armoured unit... there was a little village

called Dhuluaya fifty miles north of
Baghdad... targeted because they said they
were in cahoots with Al Qaeda... they
wouldn't give any information... so the
Americans threatened to flatten their
orchard...

She can see Fergus struggle with the memory.

RACHEL

What happened?

FERGUS

This old woman was hugging a tree... begging
us to stop... a young soldier, a black kid, was
ordered to get her out... he nearly had to
break her fucking arm she struggled so
much... and then the tanks came in... but you
know what got me? They were playing jazz on
their speakers... [Rachel is stunned] ...then all
those roots torn up... and that old woman's
wails... the black kid tried to hide it but he
had tears in his eye... hard to explain
Rachel... I was so fucking ashamed of myself
for just being there... last straw... [pause] So I
got out... left the regiment.

Rachel feels for him and listens with great attention. Fergus
sips again.

RACHEL

And joined up with Haynes?

FERGUS

Not much else to do... they offered me a
fortune... my last chance to load up... they

were good to me... real professionals... not like some of the fucking cowboys out there... [pause] I'll never forget the first time I saw a shrink-wrapped package of a half million dollars... everything paid in cash... I remember the smell as we broke the plastic... made my guts tingle... so much money out there... all we talked about... corruption... backhanders... billions went missing... you have no idea...

RACHEL
Why did you split from Haynes... what happened?

FERGUS
Fancied my own firm... why not? Hired Colombians for 35 dollars a day... trained Iraqis for 150 a month... I made a fucking fortune, that's why Haynes is furious... can't stand the idea a scruff like me had an eye for the main chance as fast as him...

RACHEL
Why didn't you take on Frankie?

FERGUS
Too much work... began to cut corners... he was safer where he was... he had you to think about... I always took more chances...

RACHEL
And here you are... a big empty flat... on your own... why's that Fergus?

Fergus is quiet for a long moment.

FERGUS

I lost three of my boys in an ambush... I was
in the middle car... I got my client out...
golden rule... the 'package' comes first... I left
my boys behind... we never ever did that in
the army... At least they died quick... I
thought I was okay... but then I got a letter
from one of their mothers... that's when it all
started to fall apart... I don't give a shit about
the flat... about money... about anything... I
feel numb inside.

She takes his hand. He can't deal with the intimacy. He downs
the rest of his drink quickly.

FERGUS (CONT'D)

Got to get out of here... talked far too much
already.

16. NIGHT CLUB

Fergus and Rachel dance. For once he looks carefree.

Fergus accidentally bumps into a girl. A stout barrel-chested
figure pushes him very aggressively. Fergus stares at him for a
second, smiles, pretends to shoot him with a pistol, and then
blows him a kiss.

He goes back to Rachel. They dance like wild things; as if they
will never dance again.

17. FERGUS'S APARTMENT – NIGHT

Rachel and Fergus sit with their backs against the wall as they perch on the little camp bed. They have both taken far too much to drink and pass a half-empty bottle of wine back and forth between them.

FERGUS
[Giggling] I don't date soldiers! Remember that?... What a turn-on!

He passes her the bottle and she takes a drink.

RACHEL
[Holding his eye] And you... like an animal...

He leans across abruptly and kisses her.

A moment between them, and only then does she pull back.

FERGUS
Slap me... [hesitant, shocked] Do it.

She slaps him.

FERGUS (CONT'D)
Harder Rachel...

She does.

FERGUS (CONT'D)
Harder!

She does, and faster.

FERGUS (CONT'D)
Punch me...

She pulls back her fist, then in slow motion gently guides her fist towards his mouth. She tenderly caresses his lips with her knuckles.

He suddenly bites her finger and she lets out a gasp of pain.

FERGUS (CONT'D)
Punch me... [holding her eye] I mean it.

She punches him, but it is lightly on the cheek.

FERGUS (CONT'D)
Punch me!

She punches him full on the mouth which rocks his head. Blood trickles down over his lip.

She stares at him. She leans in and licks the blood.

They both grab each other and kiss violently for some moments.

He rips open her blouse. She rips open his shirt.

She stares at Frankie's pendant.

They pull back, shocked at themselves.

She can taste his blood and wipes it from her lip.

They both lean back on the bed.

18. FERGUS'S FLAT – MORNING

Rachel, wrapped up in an army sleeping bag in a spare room, wakens to the sound of Fergus's voice in the distance.

Sleepy and hungover, and dressed in one of Fergus's shirts as a nightgown, she moves barefooted over smooth wooden floors, to stand at the door to the study. She sees Fergus in animated conversation [via Skype] with Tommy.

> FERGUS (CONT'D)
> Fuck's sake Tommy... 1st of September I said...

> TOMMY
> Nothing happened Fergus...

> FERGUS
> They shot up a fucking taxi! There must be a report!

> TOMMY
> Well it wasn't recorded... I've checked everything...

> FERGUS
> Who else was on duty with Frankie that day?

> TOMMY
> Nelson...

> FERGUS
> Well that ties up...

> TOMMY
> And three Colombian lads...

> FERGUS
> Which ones?

TOMMY

I'll have to check again...

FERGUS

Fuck's sake! Text me their names as soon as you
find out...

TOMMY

I don't like this Fergus... I nearly got
caught...

FERGUS

I really need this Tommy... any word on
Jamie?

TOMMY

He's up a mountain somewhere... skipping
round camps fixing Jeeps... I'm trying to get a
message to him... Got to rush man...

FERGUS

Thanks Tommy... I won't forget this.

TOMMY

Neither will I...

Screen goes blank.

Fergus turns round to Rachel who's standing watching him at
the door. A moment between them.

RACHEL

Who's Jamie?

FERGUS

Old mate from the army... mechanic...
spotted a gap in the market... got his own
garage in the Green Zone... solders on armour

plate to protect vehicles… he's gone for a few
weeks to Afghanistan… he was close to
Frankie…

                    RACHEL
Who shot up a taxi?

Fergus stares at her for a moment.

                    FERGUS
Something terrible happened on the 1st of
September… two weeks before Frankie died. I
want you to meet someone… an Iraqi
musician… I'm going to meet him tonight after
his gig… Can you pretend to be a journalist?

                    RACHEL
What's going on?

                    FERGUS
I don't know Rachel… but I swear I'm going
to find out.

She studies him for a moment.

                    RACHEL
Your lip?

                    FERGUS
It's nothing.

19. VENUE – NIGHT

Scruffy, but intimate little space full of a mixture of Brits, mostly scruffy students, and what looks like Iraqi refugees. Fergus and Rachel are among them. Harim sets up his lute on a little stage. He says something in Arabic which makes half the audience laugh.

RACHEL

Did you learn any Arabic?

Fergus leans in close to her and rattles off a few lines in what sounds like decent Arabic. She is mystified and impressed.

FERGUS

[Translating] Stop. Keep back. Slow down. Out
of the car. Hands up motherfucker. And thank
you... in that order.

It wipes the smile off her face.

Harim is a sardonic presence and seems to be able to make the audience laugh easily, albeit with the darkest of humour. He has very good English, although he has a strong accent.

HARIM

...I have never been paranoid... just deeply
unpopular... First Saddam tried to kill me...
[chuckles] ...then I had a narrow escape
during the four-week bombing campaign
from the Coalition of the Willing... As I lay in
my cellar with my trembling nieces I realised I
was part of the Coalition of the Unwilling...
[more gentle tuning]... Then I survived a
rocket attack from a US gunship that
destroyed my neighbour's house and killed my

dog… A contractor once shot at me because I came too close on my bicycle… I had an appointment at my local police station… two minutes before I arrived a suicide bomber blew it up… then I went to visit my grandmother… in Fallujah!… My God!… It must run in the family… nobody liked her too… they destroyed her whole street!… One day, after the elections, when democracy arrived, I got a little note through my door from my radical friends in the Mahdi army which said if you continue to sing your unIslamic songs we are going to cut your head off… I took this very personally… Here is a little song from Mesopotamia which means 'between the rivers'… the Tigris and the Euphrates… where Homo sapiens first learned to write, count and map the stars… which anthropologists call the cradle of civilisation… in my dreams it may be once again…

Harim sings a haunting song in Arabic. Although English speakers don't understand the words [apart from a single word: Baghdad] they catch the mood from Harim's heartfelt performance and the emotional response from the audience.

Rachel notices Fergus recoil into himself. He leans his elbows on his knees and takes his head in his hands.

She puts her hand on his knee.

20. HARIM'S FLAT – DAY

Fergus, Rachel and Harim watch a few images [previously seen] from the mobile until Harim presses the pause button.

Frankie's tormented image, beside the taxi, is frozen on the TV set. Rachel, tears in her eyes, clearly stunned, stares at his image, while Harim, with several sheets of paper before him [translations of some of the recorded messages] has the mobile in his hand, on speaker.

> HARIM (CONT'D)
> There are several messages you should hear...

Harim presses a button on the mobile and translates above the sound of a desperate woman. She is half talking, half sobbing...

> HARIM (CONT'D)
> ...Please whoever you are... whoever gets this
> message... whoever has Yosuf and Malik...
> please don't hurt them... I'll sell my house...
> the car... but I beg you... please don't hurt
> them... Please phone me... They are good
> boys, students who work hard, and have done
> no harm... [struggling to control herself]...
> My only sons, my two boys... [over her
> sobs]... I beg you in the name of God please
> phone me and let me speak to them... I'll give
> you every penny I have... I'll work for the rest
> of my life...

Rachel can't stand it. She jumps up and moves to the window and stares outside.

Harim clicks the phone off and looks at her with concern. They are quiet for a few moments.

HARIM (CONT'D)

[Quietly to Fergus] Maybe you should take her
home... [Fergus nods]... Some of the rest are
more upsetting... I haven't had time to
translate all the texts... I'll contact you when I
am finished...

Fergus makes to move.

HARIM (CONT'D)

We have to phone this woman... put her out of
her misery.

RACHEL

[Struggling to control herself] She hasn't given
up... has she... her only sons...

FERGUS

[To Harim] I give you my word we will phone
her... but we still don't know for certain what
happened... maybe they got to a hospital...
kidnapped, in prison... who knows out
there...

RACHEL

[Snapping] They were obviously murdered!
Left for dead at the side of the road!

She charges out of the room.

FERGUS

I'll phone you Harim...

HARIM

She's probably right.

He runs after Rachel.

OUTSIDE THE FLAT:

Several flights of stairs and pounding feet.

Fergus bounds down the stairwell chasing after Rachel who is a full set of stairs ahead of him.

FERGUS
Rachel... wait for me... please wait!

He sprints faster and gains on her.

FERGUS (CONT'D)
Rachel!

He leaps even faster and eventually grabs her arm as she is about to turn another bend to go down the last flight.

FERGUS (CONT'D)
Please... there's something you don't
understand!

She stops and looks at him. He lets go of her arm. She's breathing heavily.

FERGUS (CONT'D)
Look what happened to Craig!... He was
ordered to shoot... thought he saw a kid in the
car... hesitated. Boom! Blind for life! Jason lost
his legs and half his gut... will never wipe his
own arse again... split-second decisions...
fucking terrifying... us or them! And all those
hypocritical fuckers sitting in their
comfortable sitting rooms with a glass of wine
in their hands judging us because of some shite
on YouTube...

RACHEL

We just saw the film!

FERGUS

You don't know what happened before! You
don't know what happened after!

RACHEL

That boy had a mobile in his hand... not a
gun!

FERGUS

How do you think they set off the IEDs! With
mobiles...

RACHEL

What's an IED?

FERGUS

An Improvised Explosive Device! Fuck... it's
what's been killing all our lads for the last three
years! Jesus Christ Rachel!

It takes a few moments for them both to calm down. They start
to walk down the stairs again.

RACHEL

Why would there be no incident report? At
least four died and maybe more...

FERGUS

To avoid a scandal... If they get a cowboy
reputation it could jeopardise contracts worth
millions...

RACHEL

And what about those poor people in the taxi?

FERGUS

Over a million dead! Do you think anyone
gives a flying fuck about one stupid taxi driver
and a nosey kid?

Rachel is stunned. Silence.

RACHEL

Maybe Frankie? He seemed to care…

Again, silence between them. Fergus receives a text.

FERGUS

[Quiet now] From Tommy… names of the
Colombians on duty with Frankie when the
taxi was shot up…

Rachel takes the phone and her face colours.

RACHEL

Same boys who were killed with Frankie on
the 17th.

FERGUS

Are you sure? [She nods] Fuck… Nelson… the
only survivor…

RACHEL

[Increasingly emotional]… Who shot up the
taxi… who is he?

FERGUS

Macho arsehole… we were in the paras
together before I joined the SAS…

RACHEL

Maybe it's a coincidence… but I'm going to
the police right now!

Fergus grabs her.

FERGUS

Can you imagine the plods in Baghdad? These
bastards will dribble rings round them...

RACHEL

I'll create such a stink they'll have to
investigate properly! I'll contact my MP, every
newspaper in the country! I'll write to...

FERGUS

Please Rachel!... Calm down... Please! [After a
moment she does] Remember the Iraqi picked up
by soldiers in Basra? [She shakes her head] Beaten
to death! Ninety-three injuries... still they got
off... they close ranks... always have, always will.

Rachel is tearful and resigned.

RACHEL

What can we do?

FERGUS

Give me a little time Rachel...

RACHEL

[Stopping in her tracks] Fuck! Oh my God...

FERGUS

What is it?

RACHEL

Walker... at the funeral... asked me about an
Iraqi mobile... said Frankie had borrowed it
from one of the drivers and forgot to give it
back...

FERGUS

Bastard. He knows.

21. CAR PARK, HOTEL

Fergus drives his sports car at speed towards an hotel car park as Rachel sits beside him. They pull into a busy car park.

Fergus and Rachel sit together, waiting. She holds two new Nokia mobile phones in her hand and a device she doesn't recognise.

RACHEL

Was he nervous?

FERGUS

Shitting himself...

RACHEL

Will he turn up?

FERGUS

I know he will...

She looks at him suspiciously and is about to say something.

FERGUS (CONT'D)

Don't ask Rachel.

He takes one of the phones from her.

FERGUS (CONT'D)

[Indicating the other in her hand] Put that one on 'silent'.

She does. Fergus dials the number of the phone in her hand.

FERGUS (CONT'D)

Is it working?

She puts it to her ear.

FERGUS (CONT'D)
I'll hide it in his car. [She looks amazed as he
takes it from her.] I'll put mine on mute.
Sometimes the simplest things work best.

He takes the other gadget from her.

RACHEL
What's that?

FERGUS
A tracking device... nothing fancy... buy it
over the counter... [noticing a car pull in]
there he is there...

They watch Walker arrive and park his enormous brand new
4x4 and head towards the hotel.

RACHEL
I don't know if I can bear this again...

Fergus glances at her.

Walker disappears into the hotel.

Fergus gets out of his car and casually walks over to Walker's
vehicle.

Rachel watches him skilfully pick the lock of Walker's 4x4.

He plants the mobile behind the sun screen above the passenger
seat.

He gets out of the car and ducks down to stick the magnetic
tracking device under the boot.

22. HOTEL

Fergus and Rachel sit in close to Walker who speaks quietly, but with conviction, in a quiet corner of the lounge.

Fergus sips soda water.

> WALKER
> We got army intelligence overnight... they suspected suicide bombers were going to use taxis... [he hands a copy of the report to Fergus]... I spoke to the entire team... I put Nelson on as 'trunk monkey'... rear gunner... and really warned him... he's rough, but he doesn't panic... they got to Route Irish and this taxi with shaded windows started closing in far too close... our Jeep moved from inside lane to outside lane... the taxi followed... they tried to pull away but the taxi was on their tail... cat and mouse for over a kilometre... Nelson was sure they were closing in... one of the Colombian boys was screaming at Nelson to fire warning shots... things got tense... he fired... it didn't pull back... Nelson had no option... he took out the taxi...

> RACHEL
> What about Frankie?

> WALKER
> He wasn't himself the last month... went crazy. He forced the driver to stop and he ran back to the taxi... he risked his own life and the entire team... Nelson wanted him sacked... but Frankie was right. He opened the taxi

door and the driver fell out... dead... so was the passenger... there were another two in the back... the kid died in front of his eyes... It was a terrible mistake done in the heat of the moment...

RACHEL

What did you do?

Walker looks around him.

WALKER

I'm risking my entire career here... [pause] I should have gone through the channels... Frankie was beside himself, especially for the kid in the back... [Rachel struggles]... We were all gutted... he suggested compensation... we all agreed... chipped in ourselves without telling anyone outside Iraq...

FERGUS

Does Haynes know?

WALKER

I began to write my report... then the news came in... a suicide bomber in a taxi blew up a vehicle... four contractors killed on Route Irish... I tore up the report and told no one... It wasn't going to bring the Iraqis back... I didn't want to see Frankie fired, my boys blacklisted for one mistake... Frankie was in a terrible state... Did he phone you that night Rachel?

She nods her head. She is overcome.

WALKER (CONT'D)
I phoned my wife that night too... talked for
hours...

Rachel's head goes down.

Walker can feel Fergus's eyes burn through him. He takes his
Blackberry out of his pocket, finds a number and rings.

WALKER (CONT'D)
I went with Hakim and paid the taxi driver's
family in cash... we found the other family
too... Hakim set it up and organised it all...
Speak to him Fergus... [Phone connects]
Hakim!... Walker here... I'm in the UK with
Fergus... he's got a few questions for you...

He hands the phone to Fergus who takes it and walks off.

Walker looks genuinely forlorn.

WALKER (CONT'D)
It's a filthy business...

A few moment's silence.

RACHEL
Did you bring the photo of Frankie's vehicle?

He stares at her for a moment, digs it out of his folder, and
hands it over.

WALKER
We got it towed back to base...

Rachel examines the burnt out vehicle photographed back at
the base. She can feel her eyes fill up again.

Fergus comes back and hands Walker back his Blackberry.

FERGUS

It's true... they paid the families.

Rachel hands Fergus the photograph of Frankie's vehicle. He stares at it for a few moments as Walker pays sharp attention to them both.

WALKER

Frankie was too good for Iraq. He should have
left it to cynics like me.

RACHEL

I think I owe you an apology.

Walker shakes his head.

Fergus stares at Walker.

FERGUS

Did anyone else die that day?

WALKER

It happened on Route Irish... a packed
road... they had to get out quickly... but not
that I know of...

A long moment between them.

WALKER (CONT'D)

Got to go if you don't mind... my daughter's
birthday... missed the last three... Phone me if
you have any more questions...

They shake hands and they watch him leave.

RACHEL

He's telling the truth.

FERGUS

What about the two boys on the bike?

RACHEL

Maybe he believed they were setting off a
bomb too?

Fergus springs up.

FERGUS

Come on…

23. CAR PARK

Fergus and Rachel sit in the car as Fergus holds his mobile
between them. They are deadly silent as they listen to Walker's
voice as he speaks to someone on his mobile.

WALKER'S VOICE

Think it was okay… she believed me that's for
sure… no… he wasn't drinking… mineral
water the whole time… looks in good shape…
he's a hard fucker… He spoke to Hakim…
that was a good fucking idea man… The
mobile… I don't think they've got it… would
have asked more questions… Let's keep cool…
maybe we've knocked it on the head… best if
he gets done and they send him to prison for a
couple of years…

Rachel glances at Fergus as Walker chuckles on the phone.

WALKER'S VOICE (CONT'D)

Are the contracts done?… Great… we're on a
roll… have you got a date? Excellent… the day
before I leave… yeah… we've got to celebrate!

Champagne all round!... No... out of
Heathrow. When do you go to Washington?...
Phone you tomorrow... Cheers Andrew...
[Fergus and Rachel catch each other's eye]
...thanks for the call...

Silence for a second and then the sound of a car radio and
BBC 2 jingle.

Fergus clicks off the phone.

RACHEL

Bastards...

Fergus's phone bleeps with a message. He checks it.

FERGUS

Great... Peggy... Green Zone, Baghdad...
says she has something... [Pause] Have you
checked his emails yet?

She shakes her head. Silence. She looks upset.

RACHEL

I'm scared of what I might find... [pause]...
just seeing his name hurts so much.

Fergus looks like he's about to say something but she cuts him
off.

RACHEL (CONT'D)

Don't ask... I'll have to face this.

24. FERGUS'S FLAT

PEGGY's bright face fills the computer screen as she talks to Fergus on Skype.

> PEGGY
>
> Nelson was smashed... 'Fucking goody two
> shoes this!... Florence Nightingale that... why
> don't you go shag a Rag Head if you love
> them so much Florence'... kept calling Frankie
> 'Florence'... shouting across the bar... on and
> on... Frankie never said a word... and then he
> started on about a mobile... 'Where's the
> fucking mobile Florence?... I saw you pick it
> up'... Frankie still ignored him... then Nelson
> grabbed him by the collar... 'Where's the
> fucking mobile Florence?'... That's when
> Frankie hit him... he went flying over a table
> and Christ knows how he got up again... 'I'm
> going to kill you you cunt' he shouted... and
> ran at him with a bottle... Frankie ducked and
> whacked him again... smashed his face up
> proper... Walker came in with a bunch of the
> boys and managed to drag Nelson out of there
> screaming blue murder... Then the weird bit...
> I went to clean the toilets that night... and
> there it was, written on the wall... 'Florence
> you are a dead girl!!' It scared me Fergus... he
> really meant it.

There is the sound of someone shouting 'Peggy' off screen.

> PEGGY (CONT'D)
>
> Shit... got to run Fergus, there's my car... I'll
> try and get Jamie for you... he's still not back.

FERGUS

Thanks Peggy... take good care love... keep
safe.

Fergus's face hardens as he stares out over the city. He's already
dialling on his mobile. The phone connects, but it is an
answering machine.

FERGUS (CONT'D)

Tommy... Fergus... I need to know where
Nelson was the day Frankie died... I need to
know when he's coming home... phone me
man... as soon as you can...

He switches off the phone, his mind racing.

25. FERGUS'S LOCK-UP

Fergus, dressed in a tracksuit, pounds a punchbag dangling
from the ceiling with kicks and punches. He moves with great
speed and power – his face in total concentration. He pushes
himself to the limit as he talks to himself between grunts and
blows.

FERGUS

That's for Frankie... another one... another
one... take that you fucker... and that... and
that... and fucking that!

LATER: In silence he oils a stubby hand gun and checks that it
is in perfect working order.

26. CRAIG'S HOUSE – NIGHT

Fergus lies back on Craig's settee. It's the middle of the night but he's wide awake.

He hears a shout, and tenses.

He gets up, and notices Craig's light is on. He hears him mumble and then shout out again. A nightmare. He peeks into his bedroom. Craig twists and turns in a troubled sleep, under a bright light he has forgotten to turn off.

Fergus sits on the edge of his bed for a long moment. He takes his mate's hand and tries to comfort him.

> ### FERGUS (CONT'D)
> It's okay Craig... sleep man... I'm right beside you mate... shhh... easy.

He seems to calm. Fergus stares at his mate's mutilated face as Craig begins to breathe more regularly again.

He cradles his mate's hand and then leaves again. Light off. Darkness.

27. RACHEL'S FLAT – DAY

Rachel, her face tense and emotional, stares at the computer screen.

She puts a hand to her mouth.

> ### RACHEL
> My God...

She scrolls through the names of emails received.

RACHEL (CONT'D)
[Whispers to herself] Marisol... Marisol...
Marisol... Rachel... Rachel.

We only see her face. She bites her lips as she scrolls down over more messages we can't see.

Her eyes dart from one message to the next as she reads at speed. Her distress grows.

Her eyes fill with tears. At last she starts to cry quietly to herself.

She stands up and moves to the mantelpiece. She stares at the photo of them both at the half marathon.

28. FERRY OVER THE MERSEY TO BIRKENHEAD

Fergus and Rachel are on the top deck of the ferry, windswept, looking out over the water towards the sea, with Liverpool behind them.

FERGUS
I feel close to him out here... we used to skip school... get a bottle of Buckfast... and come up here on deck... nobody to hassle us... Used to pretend we were on our way to New York or Rio... so many daft plans... [pause] I cross every day Rachel... back and forth... back and forth... fucking calms me down... trying to catch how we were before all this...

Rachel looks at him.

RACHEL
I can't believe I hit you like that... don't know what got into me...

FERGUS

You'd be amazed at what we can do…

Fergus looks at her for a moment. Her fragility and honesty get
to him.

FERGUS (CONT'D)

Did you open his emails?

RACHEL

[Struggling] Lots to Marisol… can see why
you liked her… [pause]… intimate talk… dirty
stuff too… [hurt]… he didn't do that with
me… sounds like a different man…

FERGUS

That's how we are… I'm different with you
than anyone else… when we get off this boat…
separate… I'll be different than I am now…
you too Rachel… He talked about you all the
time… that's the truth…

RACHEL

He was missing you… missing me… his
frustrations at work… sent out to the airport
three times in his last week and nobody turned
up…

This gets Fergus.

FERGUS

Three times! Route Irish… like a shooting
gallery!

RACHEL

Pissed off with one of the vehicles too… said it
wasn't safe…

FERGUS

Which one?

She shrugs.

RACHEL

…and furious about Nelson… he said
something one morning at breakfast that really
upset Frankie… I didn't understand it…
[pause, confused] 'Going to get myself a Rag
Head'.

She waits for his answer.

FERGUS

Kill an Iraqi.

RACHEL

What?! 1st of September! The day Nelson shot
up the taxi! His mate had been killed in Basra
the day before… [struggling with incredulity]
That can't be true… don't tell me that…

She stares at Fergus, and knows the answer.

RACHEL (CONT'D)

My God… what kind of place… Frankie had
a huge bust-up with Walker… nearly came to
blows… an argument over Nelson, but no
details… must have been about the taxi I
suppose… [pause] Do you think they could
have…

She stops as she sees the look in Fergus's eye.

RACHEL (CONT'D)

You won't do anything crazy Fergus…

She grips his hand.

> RACHEL (CONT'D)
> Promise me Fergus... Promise me! Or I won't
> tell you another thing!

> FERGUS
> I don't make promises any more Rachel...
> only to Frankie...

> RACHEL
> You're scaring me Fergus.

29. ROAD, OUTSKIRTS OF LIVERPOOL

Fergus drives his sports car, one eye on the road, one eye on the tracking device which indicates the direction of the car he follows.

The tracking device informs him he should take a right-hand turn. He does so and sees a sign for a golf club.

He pulls into the car park.

30. GOLF COURSE

Walker, by himself, tees off on a quiet course with a number one wood. He's satisfied by his fine drive and the prospect of a relaxing round.

In the middle of the deserted fairway, as Walker pulls an iron from his trolley and is about to address the ball, he becomes aware of a determined figure, in his line of fire, walking towards him at speed.

He can feel his stomach tighten as he recognises Fergus marching closer. He nervously glances around him. There is nobody else in sight.

Fergus marches up to him, his face expressionless.

FERGUS
'Florence... you are a dead girl.' Does that
ring any fucking bells?

Fergus grabs Walker's trolley and starts pulling it. He turns
round and waits for a nervous Walker, who reluctantly joins
him. They walk up the fairway together.

Further along: they talk side by side.

WALKER
I didn't lie... just didn't tell you... scared of
what you might do...

Fergus stares at him, weighing up every word.

WALKER (CONT'D)
Nelson attacked Frankie one night in Peggy's
bar... Nelson accused Frankie of picking up a
mobile from some Jacky... convinced he'd
filmed him on Route Irish... I don't know if
it's a lot of paranoid shit or not but that's what
Nelson said... Do you know anything about
this?

FERGUS
No.

WALKER
I fired Nelson the following day after the
fight... but he threatened to go public...
expose what happened with the taxi...

FERGUS
All your fancy contracts... up in smoke.

WALKER

[Nodding] I had to eat my words... take him
back.

FERGUS

Why didn't you just pay him off?

WALKER

I tried to... he just laughed... he loves it out
there... all the gear... the adrenalin... showing
off to journalists... but best of all he loves to
rub my face in it after I tried to fire him...

FERGUS

Do you think he slotted Frankie?

WALKER

He hated Frankie... he's got a temper... but I
don't see how he could have done it... I
honestly think Frankie was in the wrong place
at the wrong time... Route Irish.

Fergus stares at Walker for a few seconds.

WALKER (CONT'D)

I'm not hiding anything... honestly.

FERGUS

What are you going to celebrate? With
Haynes.

Walker is stunned. Nervous in the extreme. He's thinking
desperately.

FERGUS (CONT'D)

Best not to lie to me again.

WALKER

Promise you'll never say you got this from
me... [Fergus just stares] A take-over... [pause]
Uriel Security... desperate to get our access to
Special Forces... you know Haynes's contacts...
Mr Network... he knows everyone here...

FERGUS

And Washington. Should be a nice trip.

Again Walker is stunned.

FERGUS (CONT'D)

You're all going to make a fortune... aren't
you?

Fergus stares at him for a few seconds and then walks off.

31. FERGUS'S FLAT

Fergus, shocked, stares at Tommy's battered face on his
computer screen [on Skype again]. His face is black and blue,
swollen, and it looks like his nose has been smashed.

FERGUS

Is it broken?

TOMMY

[Touching his face tenderly] Yeah... I don't
know who fucking told him... but he knew I'd
been asking questions... he kicked my door
down in the middle of the night... dragged me
out... I got such a kicking... I've got two ribs
done too...

FERGUS

I'm so sorry mate... I'm really sorry...

TOMMY

He asked about a mobile... I didn't know what
the fuck he was talking about!... He thought I
was lying... nearly fucking strangled me
man... [opening his shirt to reveal bruising
round his neck] could hardly breathe...
thought he was going to kill me.

FERGUS

I'll make this up Tommy... [Pause] Did you
manage to check the rota?

Silence.

TOMMY

I got fired Fergus... Nelson told them I was
digging around, checking records... I'm really
fucked man... [Pause] I had to tell Nelson it
was for you... no choice man... he's on the
war path and heading home...

FERGUS

Did you get his address?

Tommy hesitates.

TOMMY

Yeah... I'll text it. You better be careful man.

32. MANCHESTER AIRPORT

NELSON [a powerful thick-set man, late thirties, with crew
cut] arrives with a huge rucksack dangling easily from one
shoulder. He has short sleeves to show off the fruits of his hours
in the gym. He has a mobile to his ear as he leaves the airport
and heads towards the taxi rank.

NELSON

...No... just the usual shit... Yeah... I'm up
for that... sounds like fun... need to kick back
man... yeah came back early... something
needs sorting... I want a hand... you and your
two best boys who can keep their mouths
shut... thanks man...

33. FERGUS'S FLAT

Fergus stands on his balcony looking out over the Mersey. His
phone rings and he answers.

FERGUS

[Only his side of the conversation] In
Liverpool... well well... the Beatles tour again?
[Pause as he listens] Questions... well... just a
few... no more bullshit... you name it, I'll be
there.

34. SMART BAR, HOTEL, LIVERPOOL

Fergus walks into a plush corporate setting mostly full of
businessmen and women. He notices Haynes at the bar and
walks towards him. Haynes greets him warmly and shakes his
hand.

HAYNES

Let's take a seat... cards on the table Fergus.
What do you want to drink?

FERGUS

Water.

HAYNES

Good. Taking care of yourself.

QUIET CORNER: Fergus and Haynes sit opposite each other. Haynes is as convincing and as passionate as ever.

                    HAYNES (CONT'D)
        …even after the take-over I'll still be at the
        heart of it… can hire who I like… major plans
        Fergus… want to get into the meaty stuff and
        leave the dross behind… blue chip clients and
        governments… consultancy, analysis and risk
        management… kidnap negotiation and large-
        scale insurance fraud… mine clearance and
        country reconstruction… I'm looking at the
        big picture… we can be more efficient than
        NGOs and take more off standing armies…
        get the work done, security on the ground… if
        I had one good regiment of top-class boys
        hand picked – I mean the best – we could sort
        out Darfur and leave the UN and their sexual
        molesters behind in the shit where they
        belong! That's how big we're thinking… I
        mean BIG… Iraq is dust… pastures new…

He sips his drink. Fergus just watches.

                    HAYNES (CONT'D)
        I need people like you Fergus… or if I can be
        frank… like you were…

This strikes Fergus. He smiles.

                    FERGUS
        [As if savouring it, to himself] Like I was…

                    HAYNES
        One of the best… Why don't you come
        back… work with me?… [Pause] I've got a

good guy I see myself sometimes… not a
shrink… an executive counsellor… we are so
driven sometimes we lose perspective… what
do you think?

Long pause.

FERGUS
What about Nelson?

HAYNES
[Force] Forget him!… Small fry.

FERGUS
Do you think he slotted Frankie?

Haynes hesitates and looks around him.

HAYNES
Nelson talked about shooting a Rag Head that
morning… I believe that… he was an
arsehole… Frankie was convinced it was
murder… The Colombian boys with him said it
was a fair call… what can I say?… Frankie
wasn't at his best after you left… had a few close
shaves and he was burnt out… Nelson said
Frankie had picked up a mobile from a
witness… sounds a bit far-fetched to me… [He
studies Fergus's eyes]… Anyway, what would
Frankie do? He'd throw it in the river…
wouldn't he? [Waiting for an answer but nothing
comes]… Once a soldier, always a soldier.

FERGUS
If there was a mobile… and Nelson couldn't
get it off him… maybe he went for Frankie?

HAYNES

I've asked around Fergus... believe me...
Nelson was close to that dodgy driver he had
with the limp... they called him Mad Max
because of the way he drove... remember him?
[Fergus nods] Ex-police... corrupt as hell...
two days before Frankie died Nelson spent the
day with him...

Fergus's eyes flash and he is fully alert again.

FERGUS

Where?

HAYNES

Green Zone. They left together... we owed
him a month's wages plus bonus... we never
saw him again... why was that? Could he have
done Frankie on Nelson's say so? Or was he
kidnapped, blown up or joined relatives in
Jordan? Who fucking knows in Baghdad?
There's just no way to be sure...

Fergus has that look in his eye.

FERGUS

Says who?

Long moment between them.

HAYNES

Leave it Fergus... or you'll end up a poisoned
old sod rotting away in some filthy bedsit... or
worse.

They stare at each other for a long moment.

Haynes doesn't back down. Fergus gives in first. He seems to relax for the first time.

> FERGUS
>
> Maybe you were right... just wrong place...
> wrong time...

> HAYNES
>
> I believe so Fergus... I know we can work
> together again... Call me.

35. CRAIG'S HOME – DAY

Fergus lies out on Craig's settee.

Craig sits on a comfy chair. They sip from cans. Quietness between them.

Fergus stares at Craig's marked face and dead eyes.

> FERGUS
>
> Know what he said... 'I want you back'...
> [slowly]... 'the way you were'... Can you
> remember, Craig, 'how we were'?

Craig stares into the darkness for a long moment. As if he hadn't heard. At last he shakes his head. He sips a little more from his can.

> FERGUS (CONT'D)
>
> [Forlorn] Neither can I.

36. RACHEL'S FLAT – DAY

Rachel pushes open the door to her flat. The lock is broken. She's very frightened and on the alert. She tentatively opens the sitting room door.

> **RACHEL**
> My God.

The place has been torn apart by thieves. Her eyes flick everywhere. She looks to the mantelpiece and her mouth goes to her hand.

The little vase with Frankie's ashes lies smashed on the ground, and his ashes are scattered on the floor.

She kneels before them and begins to cry.

37. FERGUS'S FLAT – LATER

Nelson, plus three well-built men wearing plastic gloves, move methodically through the apartment and search every corner. There's not much to overturn.

> **MAN 1**
> Sure the cunt lives here?

The phone starts ringing. There is a look between them, but then they continue with the search.

The answering machine clicks on and Nelson pays close attention. An upset female voice.

> **RACHEL'S VOICE**
> Fergus… I've tried your mobile… where the
> hell are you?…Phone me! Someone's broken
> into my flat… a total mess… they even
> upturned Frankie's ashes…

MAN 2

Ah that's what it was!

Chuckles of bad taste among them.

RACHEL'S VOICE

Nothing stolen... you know what that means...
don't you?... I'm scared Fergus... phone me
for God's sake...

As the answering machine clicks off Nelson examines the
machine. He clicks back over old messages.

CRAIG'S VOICE

It's me... Fancy a run tonight... got to get out
of this house man I'm going crazy... Jamie left
a message... he wants to see you... give me a
phone...

Another message, and the sound of a foreign accent that excites
Nelson even more.

HARIM'S VOICE

This is Harim calling for Fergus...

NELSON

A fucking Rag Head...

HARIM'S VOICE

...I have finished all the translations...
including text messages...

Nelson's eyes light up.

NELSON

That's our man... he's got the fucking mobile.

HARIM'S VOICE

Call me at 07700900218... Maybe you could
call round to my flat if you want...

NELSON

Fucking good idea Rag Head! [taking out his
phone, texting, and mouthing out the words]
Fergus here... mobile stolen... can you text
address again?

The men look at each other and begin to chuckle.

38. STAIRWELL INTO HARIM'S FLAT

The same four men, now wearing masks, line up outside
Harim's flat. They carry baseball bats.

The ring the doorbell. Harim opens the door and the men
burst in.

Using the same dramatic procedure as the military they make
Harim and his two terrified flatmates, a man and a woman,
kneel on the floor in the hall.

Nelson and co. are rough but professional. They tie up the
occupants with plastic cuffs and stand over them.

NELSON (CONT'D)

Which one is Harim?

The flatmates whisper among themselves in Arabic which
infuriates Nelson. He smashes his baseball bat against a vase
and mirror in a fury.

NELSON (CONT'D)

Okay... I'll break your legs one by one till I
find out! Who's first?

Momentary silence between them. Nelson picks one at random and then pulls back the bat as if to strike.

HARIM

It's me!... I'm Harim. What do you want?

Nelson, accompanied by one of his team, roughly grabs him and drags him by the hair into the sitting room.

The other two, on their knees, listen to the shouts from inside as they kneel before the other two masked men.

Vicious shouts and threats come from next door but the words can't be heard. The flatmates are terrified as they hear a blow and Harim scream in pain.

MASKED MAN 1

Brings back memories eh?

The other masked man laughs.

Harim shrieks again as the shouts get louder. The woman begins to cry as she can hear Harim obviously being thrown around the room.

NELSON

[Screaming] Where's the fucking mobile?

Harim crashes against the door; more moans. It sounds like his head is being smashed against the door.

Another terrible wail from Harim.

The other Iraqi in the hall closes his eyes and begins to pray in a quiet whisper. It infuriates Masked Man 1. He boots the kneeling man full on the face knocking him out instantly. He lies there without moving.

The woman begins to scream in a panic.

Masked Man 1 grabs her by the hair and screams at her.

MASKED MAN 1
Shut the fuck up you stupid cow!

39. HOSPITAL – DAY

Fergus marches along a hospital corridor, almost knocking swing doors off their hinges as he makes his way along. He approaches Rachel who is already talking to a nurse. Behind them he can see Harim propped up on bed with his eyes closed. His Iraqi flatmate, AVIN, is by his side. His arm is in plaster, his face is badly swollen and he has a bandage round his forehead.

RACHEL
[Shocked and pale] They broke his arm in two
places... he's had sedation and is a bit mixed
up... they've given us five minutes...

FERGUS
Did he recognise them?

RACHEL
Wearing masks and gloves... [She holds up a
plastic cuff] Tied them up with these...

Fergus takes the familiar cuffs in his hands.

FERGUS
Nelson... he just got back.

Fergus approaches the bed and nods at Avin who whispers something in Arabic to Harim. He responds immediately and opens his eyes. [Upset and emotional.]

FERGUS (CONT'D)

I'm sorry Harim…

HARIM

I tried… [shaking his head]… but I had to tell
them where it was… [indicating]… they
threatened to hurt Avin… I had a copy on a
computer… but they smashed that too… on a
disc… they found them all… gone… I've been
a fool.

He shakes his head in disgust.

FERGUS

It's not your fault Harim…

HARIM

It is my fault! I should have put the footage on
the net!… I'm ashamed of myself… I needed
the money…

FERGUS

I'll pay you Harim… don't worry…

He gets agitated and Avin tries to calm him.

HARIM

Should have listened to my heart!

AVIN

[Arabic, grabbing his hand] Calm down
Harim… try and relax…

HARIM

Killers! Those that sent them… Killers! Made
fortunes! [His frustration spilling over] They
always always always get off with it… That's

what makes me mad!... I had a chance to
show what they're like... and I took the
money... I will never forgive myself!

He almost breaks down.

> FERGUS
> Please Harim... calm down... we can talk
> later...

He now looks tearful and emotional.

> HARIM
> I still have the mother's name and number...

> FERGUS
> Where Harim?

> HARIM
> [Pointing to his head] In here... You promised
> to phone her...

> FERGUS
> I give you my word... [pause] I know who did
> this... and killed the boys.

> HARIM
> But can you prove it? [Holding his eye.
> Silence] I knew it... always the same.

Fergus's face hardens for a moment.

> FERGUS
> Try and rest... I'll see you soon.

40. WALKWAY BY RIVER MERSEY

Fergus and Rachel walk along by the river with the estuary beyond stretching out to the sea. Rachel is both passionate and emotional.

> RACHEL
> First Tommy... now Harim! Who next Fergus?
> Is this the way to honour Frankie? More
> innocent people being hurt? There's been
> enough hurt... enough hurt for a lifetime!

> FERGUS
> I owe Frankie...

> RACHEL
> Not this way! It's not your job! Let the police
> do it. For Christ's sake Fergus... let go!

She stops and grabs his arm to make him look at her.

> RACHEL (CONT'D)
> What would Frankie want for you?!
> Remember when you were kids... dreaming
> about the future... [to horizon] look out
> there!... I know what Frankie would want!...
> He would want his best friend, his soul mate,
> to have a life... to be happy... content... love
> someone...

Fergus looks numb. Rachel grabs his cheek.

> RACHEL (CONT'D)
> Live a life.

She holds his eye with determination – trying to give him strength.

RACHEL (CONT'D)
Forget Iraq… forget Nelson… forget the
past…

FERGUS
And Frankie?

RACHEL
You deserve another chance…

Fergus looks at her. A dreadful sadness, and then as if he's
trying to reach her.

FERGUS
No… I don't Rachel.

RACHEL
Let go…

He struggles.

FERGUS
I don't think I can…

Fergus turns away and looks out to the horizon.

41. STREET AND SUBURBAN 4X4

Nelson leaves his house in a Manchester suburb, carrying an
expensive set of golf clubs over his shoulder.

He takes out his car keys and clicks the switch. His state of the
art 4x4, top of the range, with darkened windows, flashes its
lights and the doors noisily click open.

He tosses the clubs into the boot. He gets into the vehicle and
drives off.

The short barrel of a hand gun gently presses on his temple.

FERGUS (CONT'D)

Hello 'Florence'.

Nelson's eyes flash in the mirror. He can see Fergus's face.

FERGUS (CONT'D)

Take the motorway turn-off... that's my girl.

NELSON

Fergus... what the fuck are you doing?

FERGUS

Trying to figure out why all you wankers like
golf.

42. CRAIG'S HOUSE

A tough-looking man in his late thirties with a crew cut
knocks on the door. Craig answers.

CRAIG

Who is it?

The man stares at Craig for a long moment.

MAN 1

[Scottish accent] That's an improvement you
ugly bastard!

CRAIG

Jamie yi wanker!

They embrace each other wildly.

JAMIE

Where's Fergus?... I've got to see him.

CRAIG

He's fucked off... won't answer his calls... but
he'll be back... he always comes back... Come
in yi Scottish git! We've been chasing you...
hear you were up a mountain shagging
llamas...

JAMIE

Billy goats...

Jamie follows him in and closes the door behind him.

43. FERGUS'S WAREHOUSE LOCK-UP

Fergus sits on a bench. He has a wet cloth in his hand. He snaps
it again and again. Ugly cracking sound is deeply disturbing in
the silence.

FERGUS

Time for a little 'dunk'.

It looks like he's talking to himself, and cracked up. More
snapping. He takes a few deep breaths, stretches his head from
side to side to ease the tension in his neck and then springs up.

He looks down at Nelson who is strapped and cuffed to a thick
board of wood, like an improvised bench, both ends being
supported by exercise bars. The bench [and his head] slope
down. Nelson faces the ceiling. He can barely move, but his
terrified eyes follow every move of the snapping cloth. He has
thick tape over his mouth and can hardly make a sound.

Fergus grabs one of the many watering cans he's prepared
which are laid out in a line. He looks down at Nelson.

FERGUS (CONT'D)

'No blood... no foul.'

He winks at him. It terrifies him. He struggles desperately but
cannot move.

                    FERGUS (CONT'D)
        Up to you… [snapping off the tape from his
        mouth] Where's the mobile?

                    NELSON
        This is a big mistake Fergus… I don't know
        what you're talking about…

                    FERGUS
        And you don't know who broke into Rachel's
        flat and smashed it up?

                    NELSON
        Don't know what you're talking about… I'm
        just back… let me go Fergus and you'll never
        hear from me again… that's a promise… No!

Fergus wraps the cloth round Nelson's face – his nose and
mouth – and grips it tight under his neck. He grabs a watering
can and begins to 'waterboard' him.

[As close as possible to CIA method.]

The water pours down steadily over the cloth that grips his
face. Nelson can't breathe and the panic soon manifests itself
with fluttering hands and ankles.

Fergus releases and lets the cloth loose again. Nelson coughs
and splutters as Fergus stares.

                    NELSON (CONT'D)
        I beg you man… okay… I'll tell you
        everything…

FERGUS
So it does work…

Fergus lifts the end of the board [and Nelson] up several feet so that his head is no longer inclined down and leans the edge of the board on higher spars of the exercise bars.

NELSON
I got the mobile from the Iraqi… I smashed it
to pieces and threw it in the river… it's
gone… it's all been a big mistake Fergus… I
give you my word…

FERGUS
'Get myself a Rag Head'… a mistake?

NELSON
I was fucked off Fergus… I admit it… they
slotted Danny in Basra the day before but
what I said was a stupid joke… the taxi came
too close!… Hand on heart… the other boys
were screaming at me… take it out! It was a
fucking mistake… ask Walker!

FERGUS
And the boys on the bike?

NELSON
One had a mobile!… Holding it up for a
signal to blow us up!… That's what I
thought… the other screaming instructions!…
I took them out… you would do the same…

FERGUS
Left them there to rot…

NELSON

What the fuck are you saying?... You know
what it's like... if Frankie hadn't gone nuts
nothing would have happened... just another
day in Baghdad... Frankie flipped... wanted
me nailed... an investigation!... Fuck's sake...
in Baghdad!... He'd seen too much and was
cracking up...

FERGUS

With you and Walker making his life a misery!

NELSON

No... Walker tried to make him see sense...
when that didn't work... Haynes came out...
even offered him a bunch of money... he
wouldn't budge... threatened to turn the
mobile over to some Yankee journalist... fuck
knows where he hid it... nearly looked up his
arse...

FERGUS

So you took him out?

NELSON

What!? I wasn't even in the country! I was in
Afghanistan doing a recce for Haynes...

FERGUS

Fucking liar!

Fergus drops the bench down low again so his head is inclined
down. It terrifies him.

NELSON

Telling you the truth!... Haynes wanted me
out so he could drag things out with Frankie...
wear him down... drive him out... Haynes
thought he was on the edge and might crack
up... Haynes told Walker to piss them off!

FERGUS

Who's them?

NELSON

The Colombians too... complaining about
their money... wanted the same as us... he
didn't want them blabbing either about the
taxi and fuck up his fancy contracts... So
drive the fuckers out... that was the plan!
Crap jobs... some were dodgy I'll give you
that... up and down Route Irish for nothing...
Haynes thought they would crack up or head
off home... or if they were really stupid... get
slotted... but not by us... I had nothing to do
with it Fergus...

FERGUS

Lying bastard... you threatened to take him
out!

NELSON

I give you my word... that's a lie!

FERGUS

'Florence – you are a dead girl'... Peggy's bar!
Written on the fucking wall!

Fergus snaps the cloth around him again. More water. More
horrible panic.

FERGUS (CONT'D)

Fucking liar!

Release. More coughing and spitting. He gives him time.

NELSON

I was drunk... I didn't mean it...

FERGUS

Same way you didn't mean it when you beat
up Tommy... broke the Iraqi's arm... emptied
Frankie's ashes on the floor!

NELSON

It wasn't me! No!

Fergus snaps the cloth round him again. More water. More
torture. Release.

FERGUS

Tell me the fucking truth!... How did you do
it? With that Iraqi driver... Mad Max... is
that it?

NELSON

[Pleading] I was out of the country... I can
prove it... ask Haynes!

FERGUS

I spoke to Haynes... told me you were with
Max two days before Frankie died! He was
never seen again. How much did you pay him?

NELSON

That's a fucking lie... I was out of the
country!

It infuriates Fergus who tortures him again.

More water, more desperation. Release.

Nelson gasps and chokes. Once he recovers he begins to cry.

> NELSON (CONT'D)
> What do you want me to say?... I'll say what
> you want! Yes I did it!

> FERGUS
> How!

> NELSON
> However you fucking want... I paid Max... is
> that what you want... ten thousand dollars... is
> that enough?

> FERGUS
> The fucking truth!

> NELSON
> [Sobbing] Okay... I tipped off Max... phoned
> him up as they left the Green Zone... will that
> do you? Sitting ducks on Route Irish... now
> let me go or shoot me... is that enough?

Fergus stares at him.

> FERGUS
> No... it's not enough... and never will be.

Fergus snaps.

He pulls the cloth tight over his face and begins to pour. On
and on he pours. Nelson wriggles desperately.

> FERGUS (CONT'D)
> This is for you Frankie! [Louder, bellowing]
> Frankie! Frankie! I should have been there

Frankie... I'm sorry Frankie... He'll never do
it again!... Never again will this fucking
animal hurt anyone... Hear me Frankie?! He's
a fucking goner... Never ever ever ever again!

Legs and arms quiver.

The terrible gurgling comes to an end. His twitching stops.

As if Fergus comes to. He releases his hand from underneath his
neck and drops the watering can.

He stares at Nelson's motionless body.

He appears on the brink of madness.

He collapses to a bench and lies there staring at the ceiling.

44. HARIM'S FLAT

Fergus, deathly pale, sits opposite Harim, who still looks very
tender. They both sit round a phone, with the loudspeaker on.

Fergus speaks in short dry sentences as Harim, totally stunned
by the content, translates as simultaneously as he can.

Through the speaker they can both hear sighs and sobs from
the Iraqi mother.

FERGUS
...Your two sons were shot by a British
contractor on the 1st of September on the
airport road... [terrible sobs as it sinks in,
Fergus waits for a few moments] I don't know
if it was murder, or just standard practice by a
foreign contractor who thought his life was in
danger. They died instantly and were left on
the side of the road. The 1st of September was

a bloody day in Baghdad and they must have
been lost in the chaos…

The mother cries for some time and then manages to say
something between sobs.

> HARIM
> [Translating] We tried all the police stations,
> the prisons, the morgues… but couldn't get
> round them all… [pause] What happened to
> the man who killed my sons?

> FERGUS
> [Clipped] He died, as he lived, in a violent
> incident. He was also responsible for the
> murder of my friend… a fellow contractor.

Harim's eyes flash at Fergus in amazement.

> FERGUS (CONT'D)
> I am going to ask Harim to get your personal
> details… I want to help your family… pay
> compensation for your sons…

As Harim finishes the translation the phone clicks off.

Deadly silence between them.

> HARIM
> Who are you Fergus?

> FERGUS
> One of those 'killers' you talked about… a
> vulture in Baghdad.

Fergus slaps a hefty package of cash on Harim's desk and
marches out without looking back. He runs down the stairs and
into the open air, breathing deeply.

45. FERGUS'S APARTMENT

Fergus's flat is still a mess from the break-in. Nothing has been cleared up. Fergus looks around him. He picks up a bottle of wine from the kitchen bench and opens the balcony doors. He takes a glug from the bottle.

A long-barrelled gun leans up against the wall beside the balcony doors. He picks it up and heads out onto the balcony.

From his point of view: Cross hairs on the lit-up twelve-foot Liver bird at the top of the Liver building.

He clicks the trigger. [No charge.] He notices a couple down on the old dock.

The cross hairs merge with the figure's head as he practises his profession. Click again. He focuses on another figure. Another click. Sudden animation – his gun swings in the direction of a car – he picks off the driver with a click. Another and another and then he seems to calm.

His doorbell rings and he is suddenly alert. It rings again. He hides the gun in a cupboard. Now knocking. He gets up and moves to the door, listening carefully.

Rachel's voice. It's like a blow. He slides down against the inside of the door without saying a word.

> RACHEL'S VOICE
> Fergus... are you in there? I saw your car
> outside. A neighbour let me in... I can see a
> light... open the door... Why won't you
> answer our calls? We're all worried sick... I
> know you're in there... I just know... have you
> been drinking? [Pause] If you can't speak...
> just knock the door...

137

Long silence.

Fergus lifts his hand and knocks the door just once.

> RACHEL
>
> That's good Fergus... Now open the door... I
> won't even speak if you don't want me to...
> you decide... open the door...

Fergus struggles, and hesitates.

From Rachel's point of view: There is a click as the door
unlocks.

> RACHEL (CONT'D)
>
> Good Fergus...

She pushes the door just three inches till it catches noisily on a
chain.

Fergus's point of view: He's leaning up against the wall, out of
sight, but her voice is clearer now.

> RACHEL'S VOICE
>
> [Pause] I saw Harim... he told me about the
> phone call to the mother... that took
> courage... I told him about you and Frankie...
> he's a good man Fergus... and so are you...
> Jamie came back from Afghanistan... he's at
> Craig's waiting for you... I want to see you
> too... make sure you are okay... [pause] Can
> you lift the chain?

Fergus fights to control himself.

> RACHEL
>
> Open it Fergus... [pause] I won't say
> anything...

Fergus lifts his hand up but hesitates.

RACHEL (CONT'D)
Try Fergus... I just want to hold your hand.

He looks like he's frozen.

RACHEL (CONT'D)
I'll drive you round to Craig's... cook up
something special... gentle music... relax...
you can sleep better over there... Come on...
let's get out of here. Lift the chain... [Silence]
Okay Fergus... when you're ready...
[suddenly emotional, trying to control the
tears] Oh God... I can't bear to lose you
both... that's what I'm scared of!... Phone
me... [pause]... I love you Fergus... [It hits
him like a punch.]

Fergus can hear her steps disappear.

He curls up into a tight ball on the floor and sobs between
gritted teeth.

46. ROAD, LIVERPOOL

Fergus's car overtakes another vehicle. He drives recklessly at
twice the speed limit.

He screeches past another car and then darts off at a junction.

47. CRAIG'S FLAT

Fergus, Craig and Jamie sit round a kitchen table with a cup of
tea. They are well into a long conversation. Fergus's face
darkens at each revelation. It fits the pattern.

JAMIE

...Know that look in someone's eyes... just
been too long in the place... I thought he was
cracking up or gone paranoid... but he was so
stubborn... didn't want to let them drive him
out... 'I'll go under my own steam... my last
stint... do it proper'... stuff like that...

CRAIG

Sounds like Frankie...

JAMIE

To be honest... thought he was exaggerating...
sent fourteen times to the same place in the same
month with telephone engineers... now that's
fucking dangerous if it's true... up and down
Route Irish like a yo-yo... Nelson was picking
on him at every meal time... Walker giving him
all the shitty jobs... but not getting enough time
to do his prep... that's what got him! You know
how professional he was... sometimes he'd just
come into the garage and sit there... brooding...
I tried to get him to go home but he said he had
something to sort out first... that's when he asked
me to hide the phone...

FERGUS

Did he tell you anything?

JAMIE

Cut me off... just wanted to speak to you... I
hid it in the garage for him like he asked and
then gave it to Marisol on the way back...
Fuck... couldn't believe it when I heard the
news...

Jamie looks at Fergus who stares into his cup.

> JAMIE (CONT'D)
>
> What car did he die in? Hope it wasn't one of
> mine...

> CRAIG
>
> One of the new armoured BMWs... he's got
> the photos.

Fergus takes them from his jacket.

> FERGUS
>
> This is back at base... [handing over the
> second] This one... Route Irish... just after it
> happened... you can hardly see it for the
> smoke...

Jamie examines the first one, the burnt out twisted vehicle –
unrecognisable to the normal eye.

> JAMIE
>
> BMW all right...

He examines the second. One half of the car is totally engulfed
in flames. Fergus sees Jamie's eyes flicker and then his face
change.

> JAMIE (CONT'D)
>
> No fucking way... that's the dodgy old
> Mercedes! Look... you can see there... I
> soldered on the armoured plates! Recognise
> that in my sleep... I repaired that engine a
> dozen times... I fucking told them the extra
> plate was too heavy for an old engine... I was
> so worried I'd get the blame I emailed Walker
> and copied Haynes... still got the copies! Not

to be used under any fucking circumstances...
it wasn't safe... [staring at Fergus] Got to be a
mistake... [Fergus shakes his head] He didn't
die in that Fergus... don't tell me that!

FERGUS
Nelson took him out...

JAMIE
Fucking rubbish!

FERGUS
I know...

JAMIE
He wasn't even in the country... Haynes sent
him on a job to Afghanistan...

Fergus's face colours and he shakes his head.

FERGUS
Nelson took him out! I know he did!

JAMIE
He was on the plane to Afghanistan with my
fucking mate!

Fergus jumps up from the table.

FERGUS
Tipped off his driver... ex-cop... as Frankie
left the Green Zone... Paid ten grand to have
him done!

JAMIE
Mad Max!?... With the limp?... Rubbish!

FERGUS

Nelson fucking told me!

JAMIE

Mad Max was caught coming out the Green
Zone... [gesture along his throat] Baghdad
haircut!

FERGUS

Don't believe it... he can't be dead.

JAMIE

I saw it on the fucking net with my own
eyes... screaming for his life... they cut his
throat a week before Frankie died...

FERGUS

No!

JAMIE

You'll have to do better Sherlock...

Fergus is absolutely stunned. He turns to the kitchen bench.

FERGUS

[Whispered] Ah fuck... he was telling the
truth...

Jamie looks at Craig in shock.

CRAIG

Who was telling the truth?

FERGUS

Nelson... he was telling the truth...

CRAIG

When did you see him?

Fergus slouches over the bench and looks like he's taking a turn.

FERGUS

Fuck! Nelson was telling the truth!

Jamie tries to calm him and lays a hand on his shoulder.

Fergus snaps up the photograph of the burning vehicle and thrusts it into Jamie's face.

FERGUS (CONT'D)

Are you fucking sure this was the dodgy
vehicle?

JAMIE

Bet my life on it Fergus… it was a dead cert
to conk out…

FERGUS

Fuckers… Haynes and Walker…

CRAIG

What are you talking about?

FERGUS

They set him up… they set Frankie up…

Fergus barges past Jamie and Craig and runs from the house. He sprints to the car but instead of getting in pounds the bonnet repeatedly with a savage energy.

FERGUS (CONT'D)

Fuck! Fuck! Fuck! Fuck!

48. RACHEL'S STUDIO

Fergus makes his way up a set of stairs, passing people with sports gear. He moves to a glass panel and looks onto a small studio.

Inside Rachel gives a keep fit class to the over sixties – all women. She is at the far end of the studio; she does gentle aerobic exercises to music, which they copy.

Her face is elated as she gives instructions and gentle encouragement. She looks quite beautiful; and in her element.

Fergus appreciates her, taking her all in. He continues to watch her for a few long moments; a sadness to him, as if savouring every last detail of her.

She catches sight of him. Her face changes. She runs towards the door.

Fergus is off like a shot.

Rachel sprints down the stairs as fast as she can. She bursts out into the street.

RACHEL

Fergus!

She sees his car tear out of the car park. She runs after it… but he's gone.

RACHEL (CONT'D)

Ah Fergus!

She stops and bites her lip.

RACHEL (CONT'D)

Oh God… Fergus…

49. COUNTRY HOTEL – ANOTHER DAY

Point of view from outside: Looking across a tidy lawn towards double patio doors and into a sizeable reception room. Inside there is a party of some two dozen guests who chit chat over expensive brandys and coffees. There is the faint buzz of conversation and occasional laughter.

On the back wall behind them there is a distinctive company logo and the name 'Uriel Securities'.

Haynes and Walker are in conversation with other executives.

There is the tinkle of a spoon on a cup and a polite call for silence. Haynes steps forwards and makes a few informal and entertaining remarks although the words cannot be distinguished. He introduces a fellow executive from Uriel Securities who nods politely at Haynes's generous comments.

The Uriel exec makes a few remarks in response. They hold up glasses for a toast, and then down their drinks.

Polite applause to end the reception.

50. OUTSIDE HOTEL TO CAR PARK – LATER

LOBBY:
Haynes and Walker say their goodbyes to personnel of Uriel and co. The Uriel executive and some of his team head for their expensive 4x4s in the car park surrounded by lovely gardens.

Haynes and Walker, plus a group of three, laugh together as they walk towards Haynes's silver Mercedes. Haynes and Walker approach the car door but the conversation continues for a few seconds between the friends.

A young woman hesitates. She's not sure whether to join the two going in a SUV nearby, or with Haynes and Walker. Some light-hearted banter between the group.

At last she joins Haynes and Walker.

Haynes takes out his key and clicks. The four doors open. The young woman sits in the back seat, as Haynes and Walker climb into the front.

INSIDE THE CAR:
Haynes notices an envelope taped to the centre of his steering wheel. Mystified, he rips it open and pulls out a single sheet of paper.

> HAYNES
> [Reading, confused] Wrong place... wrong time...

He and Walker look at each other for a moment as they puzzle over it. Their faces colour as the first flash of a thought hits them.

The car explodes into a fireball.

The SUV is lucky to escape.

Terrified figures sprint from the hotel and stare at the car. They are horrified to see, in the flesh, the shape of three blackened bodies slump forward in the blazing Mercedes.

This time it is not on the news.

Iraq, in an English country garden.

51. RIVER MERSEY, FERRY

Fergus, on deck, stares into the evening light. He has a phone to his ear but his words cannot be heard. He walks up and down the virtually deserted deck. He finishes his call.

After a moment he puts iPod earphones to his ear. His face seems to relax with the sound of Verdi's 'Chorus of Hebrew Slaves'. He opens his shirt and holds Frankie's pendant in his hand.

He leans on the railing and looks out to sea. He walks slowly along the railing of the ferry. He takes one last look at the outline of the city of Liverpool. He then looks up the Mersey towards the sea. Slowly he begins to head for the bow.

The chorus builds in his ears. He looks elated. He climbs over the barrier and grips on by one hand.

He snaps the chain from around his neck with the other and holds the pendant in his fist, now thrust into the air.

He looks down at the darkened waters.

FERGUS
[Whisper] Frankie…

He jumps over the side.

The music ends… the ferry sails on… just the sound of wind and water for several long moments before Fergus's voice fades in.

FERGUS'S VOICE
You looked so lovely in the studio Rachel… so
full of life… wish we could have spoken once
more… hear your voice… but I couldn't bear
it…

52. RACHEL'S FLAT

Rachel sits still on an old leather seat as tears run down her cheeks. She listens to her answering machine, and Fergus's last message continues...

> FERGUS'S VOICE (CONT'D)
> ...Hard for a civvy to understand... but I just
> wanted... [struggling for the words] my old
> self back... the way I was... I wish you had
> known me then... [Pause, change of tone] I
> sent my lawyer instructions... will you help?
> Visit Harim for me... make sure that mother
> in Iraq and her family are taken care of...
> Frankie wanted that... one in a million I
> know... criminal sons of bitches we have
> been... on the make... [Pause] I never told
> you... I once saw a child pulled from the
> rubble by her grandfather... she wore a lilac
> top... her left leg dangled from a sinew, her
> feet shredded... She points at me when I try to
> sleep...

53. BY THE RIVER MERSEY – DAY

Fergus's message continues as Rachel and Harim walk along a quiet part of the waterfront. She carries a bunch of red roses in her hand.

> FERGUS'S VOICE (CONT'D)
> I'm heading off with Frankie now... down by
> the river. We'll wait for you Rachel at the
> other side, if there is one... Best to put a mad
> dog down before it savages someone else...

> Help Craig for me… I think he'll make it if
> he gets a hand… Bye Rachel… love you…
> well almost… in my own way… Fergus…

Rachel and Harim walk along in silence, but very much together for some time. They stop at a suitable point and look out across the water in the direction of the sea and wild clouds out to the horizon.

Rachel loosens the bunch of flowers. She picks out one.

RACHEL
This one for Frankie.

She throws it into the water.

RACHEL (CONT'D)
This one for Fergus.

She hurls it into the water too.

She divides the bunch. She gives five to Harim. Five for her.

RACHEL (CONT'D)
For all who died in Iraq.

HARIM
[In Arabic] For my beloved Iraq…

They both fling their flowers into the water and watch them drift.

The River Mersey carries twelve red roses out to sea.

FADE TO BLACK.

Aftermath
Mark Townsend

They were being watched, he had figured that much. Through the trees, Tommy Shanks saw figures flashing and fading in the evening light. Then the gunfire came rolling down the hillside and ahead, in the dust, Shanks saw one of the men go down.

There was no contemplation; Shanks just went for it, racing through the enemy fire, grabbing the blood-soaked body.

Bullets kicked up puffs of dirt as the young Glaswegian dragged his friend to safety and began dressing the bullet wounds. It was 1976, and D squadron of the SAS was embroiled in the secret war against the hilltop guerrillas of Dhofar, southern Oman. In all likelihood, Shanks' bravery that evening would have been soon forgotten had it not been mentioned in dispatches. Those who served alongside Shanks were not surprised. In the clipped assessment of one officer the twenty-five-year-old was 'highly courageous', a rising star of Britain's Special Forces. But something inside the young star would change. He seemed to become poisoned from within, a cancerous fury that festered and bubbled until one night it just erupted.

Twenty-two years after Dhofar, on a warm early summer's night, Shanks arrived outside a pub in Castleford, West Yorkshire. He seemed wired. He needed to see her, try and patch things up. Things hadn't been going so well with Vicki

Fletcher of late. Just before 10pm Shanks pressed his face against the window of The Castlefields and his twenty-one-year-old girlfriend ran outside to confirm they were over. Drinkers heard them rowing in the pub car park and Shanks screaming: 'Tell me you don't love me.'

Shanks himself remembers his cone of vision shrinking, the car park narrowing to a tunnel through which a woman – the woman he loved – was running from him.

'It was like being in a video,' he said. Click. The next scene. His hand is holding a Kalashnikov AK-47 assault rifle and then its barrel moves, quickly towards the receding figure. There is the calamity of machine-gun fire. Click. A woman is frantically scrambling over car park railings. She is bleeding. The post-mortem later revealed that at this stage six 7.62 mm bullets had shattered her pelvis, ribs, lungs and right leg. Yet somehow Vicki keeps moving towards the safety of the pub. Click. The barrel swings towards her again and this time, yards from its entrance, four more bullets pass through her. Shanks sees her lying on the ground, pub regulars smothering her body with bar towels to stop the bleeding. The film stops.

Those present watched the five foot six-inch shaven-headed Shanks calmly turn and drive off in his Peugeot. Shanks was portrayed as a madman in the subsequent media outrage. But the forty-seven-year-old, on paper at least, was no such thing. In fact he was a respected anaesthetist at the local hospital and a military medic officially commended for saving lives in the furnace of battle. Shanks was no nutter and nor was his behaviour unique.

Psychiatrists who study the mental health of former service personnel saw much to recognise in Shanks' behaviour that night. They had seen it all before in war veterans; the gradual build-up of fury towards one terrible act of violence act that often led to a human death, be it suicide or murder.

They knew that those who had served in a war zone were three times more likely to develop a serious mental disorder like post-traumatic stress disorder (PTSD). They knew that those who had been to the front like Shanks had seen dreadful things during the unregulated hostilities in Oman, the brutal desert scraps of Kuwait and its burning oil fields, an apocalyptic vision that stayed with everyone who had felt its fumes choke their lungs.

One of Britain's leading consultant psychiatrists in PTSD, Dr Dafydd Alun Jones, concedes that while Shanks' case appears striking, its general components are usual for an extreme case of post-traumatic stress. Dr Jones is now monitoring similar eruptions of violence among the veterans returning from Iraq and Afghanistan. Shanks, says Dr Jones, can be interpreted as a warning, a precursor, to the problems beginning to unfold among the most recent veterans of war.

He describes the gradual unfurling of anger, the abrupt black moods, the irrational surges of fury sparked by such trivial issues as a spilt pint as being common among combat troops. Once brave soldiers become afraid to leave their homes because they cannot trust their hair-trigger tempers. Many describe themselves as 'ready to explode'. The anger mounts until it explodes like a thunderstorm clears the air. Shanks' thunderstorm morphed into a tornado that just kept spinning. Friends say Shanks had been behaving oddly during the countdown to the May night in 1998 when he killed the woman he loved.

In hindsight, like most PTSD sufferers, it seems obvious that

Shanks was a time-bomb. The competent locum anaesthetist at Pontefract General Infirmary in West Yorkshire was losing grip on reality. Those who knew him the longest had detected a lack of drive that seemed at odds with the motivated, aspirational character who excelled so precociously in the SAS. His former commanding officer was among those who noted a change. Gone was the 'enthusiastic' young man, replaced by a character he could best describe as 'confused'. But no one offered him psychiatric help, an act that may have saved his girlfriend's life.

The turning point, say friends, was the Gulf War of 1991 for which he volunteered to serve as an anaesthetist with the Royal Army Medical Corps despite resigning from the army twelve years earlier. He returned a changed man.

Perhaps it would have all been fine if Shanks had received counselling when he came back. But Shanks never got help. He was a hard man from a hard part of Glasgow. Hard men don't do therapy. His condition deteriorated. Fellow anaesthetists said he had a short temper and an even shorter fuse. Towards the end, people began referring to him as a 'Jekyll and Hyde' figure. Colleagues frequently heard Shanks and Vicki, a nurse, arguing outside the hospital accommodation blocks.

Perhaps the first indicator of Shanks' worsening mental state was the breakdown of his marriage after returning from the Gulf. Maybe his wife Julie had noticed the man she had married was fading. At this stage Dr Jones reckons Shanks would have been okay if he had received help. It is likely that before the night he shot Vicki, Shanks had entered the stage where the adrenal glands feel hot-wired and thoughts are fuddled by a surging anxiety pumping through the body. One barrister described Shanks as the owner of a 'diseased brain'.

On average it takes fourteen years for PTSD to manifest itself. Shanks killed his lover seven years after leaving a war zone, a relatively quick gestation, although more than twenty years had passed since he served in Oman.

Psychiatrists believe a broader catastrophe is looming. The NHS, already struggling to cope with the most severe cases, is unequipped to cope with the volume of cases yet to materialise among the tens of thousands of combat troops who fought in Iraq and Afghanistan. Veterans already complain that the health service fails to understand the uniquely corrosive traumas of war. The charity Combat Stress, which treats military PTSD sufferers, is recording an almost 30 per cent increase in Afghanistan veterans and is already wrestling with more than 4,500 cases.

Officially, the Ministry of Defence claims PTSD affects 3 per cent of those who served in Iraq and Afghanistan, a figure that critics say vastly underplays the issue and its potential as a real problem for the forces and, more widely, society. Closer analysis of the government's internal data, though, suggests a much bigger problem than it publicly admits. The MoD's own statistical analysis reveals that 3,970 service personnel were diagnosed with a mental disorder during the most recent twelve months for which figures are available. 'The rate of neurotic disorder, including PTSD and adjustment disorder was significantly higher' among those who had visited Afghanistan. In addition, MoD figures show the number of troops with mental health issues had risen 28 per cent on the year before. Those with PTSD had soared by 72 per cent. A new generation of men like Shanks, once brilliant men who one day might implode, is predicted. And although the effect on society of reabsorbing thousands of war veterans is hard to predict, it is certain to be profound and long-lasting.

War changes those who experience it. The mind that sees a body rupture in half from a stray rocket, a dead girl by a roadside, is likely never to forget it. It is harder to be carefree and laugh at life's absurdities when you have seen the worst there is to see. Some are better at rationalising the horrors than others. Others start to recognise the senseless nature of killings. A soldier who questions the war – the political forces responsible, the children slain during the fallout of their whims – can quickly fall apart. An unpopular war like Iraq and, to a lesser extent, Afghanistan exaggerates the sense of senseless killing among those doing the fighting, according to many veterans.

Psychiatrists appreciate that the end of the road for untreated PTSD is suicide. After the Gulf conflict, Shanks was one of four military doctors who vowed to stay in touch. They were mates who'd seen and done it all during their stint at the 32 Field Hospital in Saudi Arabia. One of them, operating theatre technician Ray Bristow, remembered Shanks as a happy-go-lucky guy, first with the wisecracks.

Bristow's own cheerful demeanour faded shortly after he came home from the Gulf. In 1996 he was diagnosed with Gulf War Syndrome, allegedly caused by the cocktail of vaccines the men took. Bristow endured deep bouts of despair and fatigue and unexplained aches and joint pains until eventually he was housebound at his home in Hull. Yet history would prove that Bristow was the lucky one of the four. Two of them developed depression and killed themselves. By the time Shanks murdered Vicki he too was fighting suicidal thoughts.

No one knows how many Iraq and Afghanistan veterans have committed suicide. Many leave the armed forces and kill themselves without their military experience being considered a factor. The only available figures indicate that around 100 veterans who served in Iraq or Afghanistan may have committed suicide or are suspected of having killed themselves. The suicide toll is expected to rise once a number of inquests are complete. A recent conversation with Combat Stress welfare officer Stephen Pettitt offered an insight into the unknown toll of military suicides. Pettitt described how in the previous fortnight he had lost two clients out of the blue. One was a woman who had left the RAF, started a course at university and seemed to be getting her life on track after a tough period. One evening, without warning, she walked down to the local Hampshire stables and overdosed. The other was an Iraq veteran who appeared to be overcoming his demons when one afternoon he complained to his wife of severe stomach pains. He began bleeding heavily from his posterior at 4pm and arrived in hospital an hour later. The doctors couldn't stop the flow of blood. By 8pm he was dead. The deceased was diagnosed with irritable bowel syndrome which can frequently be a symptom of PTSD, although none had ever seen a case so severe. 'It's always the ones you least expect,' said Pettitt.

One seldom discussed aspect of recent conflicts is their tendency to kill more soldiers once they are officially over. The first Gulf War saw twenty-four British soldiers killed in action yet the MoD admit that the number of veterans who have since committed suicide is at least seven times higher. Similarly the Falklands conflict killed 255 soldiers but at least 264 have since committed suicide, irrefutable proof that war – the duty of killing people – exerts a terrible burden on the mind.

Psychiatrists say the reason some are more susceptible to conditions like PTSD depends on a combination of factors.

Recruitment strategies often focus on taking individuals from the ragged fringes of Britain, the sink estates, the obsolete ports, hauling men from poverty and broken families, men who embrace the belonging of the army but are prepared for little else if they dare leave. Traumatic childhoods can also exaggerate the likelihood of developing PTSD. Shanks, for instance, was ten when he found his epileptic father, a sawmill labourer, dead at home. In many ways Shanks' backstory is typical. One of eight children from a tough district of Glasgow, his mum drank heavily after her husband's death and became aggressive to her offspring. Shanks left home as soon as he could, excelling quickly within the structure of the military.

By the time he was 18, eighteen months after signing up, Shanks became the youngest soldier for a decade to pass the strenuous SAS selection course. It is when men like Shanks leave their surrogate family that usually the problems kick in. The heavy drinking culture can spill over into life on the outside. Like most, Shanks enjoyed a pint. Even after killing Vicki he pulled over at a nearby pub for half a lager. But often soldiers drink because they need to. Self-medication they call it. Experts argue that alcohol abuse in the armed forces is out of control, a central factor in the high incidence of mental breakdown. One recent study concluded as many as 23,000 members of the armed forces – around one in seven – are drinking 'hazardous and harmful' levels. Those sent to the frontlines of Iraq and Afghanistan are 22 per cent more likely to develop a drink problem than those not deployed. Drinking invariably accentuates the black moods, the violent outbursts. Ultimately many ex-servicemen are locked up. After Shanks was caught and placed on trial, the jury rejected his claims of

PTSD and diminished responsibility, declaring him guilty of murder instead of manslaughter at Sheffield Crown Court in April 2000.

Shanks might not have expected sympathy for committing his appalling act but surely he warranted treatment for his mental condition. Instead he was ordered to the second home for Britain's war veterans: prison. Inside the UK penal estate Shanks would have found men whose past he recognised. A 2009 study by the National Association of Probation Officers found 8,500 former veterans were inmates, 8.5 per cent of the total prison population and almost as many British troops as are in Afghanistan. Another group, Veterans in Prison, calculated the figure at 9,000, a proportion comparable to the hordes of former veterans incarcerated within the US penitentiary system. Most alarming, though, was a pilot study by Kent Police last year. The officer supervising the research expected to find, at most, 30 veterans a month passing through the force's custody suites. He recorded 22 on the first day. Over three months during the summer of 2010, Kent Police arrested 232 ex-service personnel, 73 for violent offences. Almost 4 in 10 were unemployed. Kent Police is one of 34 forces in England and Wales, the potential but unquantified number of veterans being arrested per year is almost certain to run into the tens of thousands.

Those who visit Shanks in prison claim that even now, after more than a decade inside, he is not getting proper treatment or counselling for his condition, nullifying any hopes of rehabilitation. In 2008 a senior judge ruled Shanks should stay locked up for at least eighteen years. Critics believe the volume of veterans in prison stems partly from an unacknowledged state policy based on simple economics. It is easier and cheaper to spend the £38,000 required to keep an inmate for a year than stumping up the cost of rehab and the intensive long-term use of specialist experts that are needed to tackle severe PTSD. Plus it negates the risk and subsequent cost of re-offending. The government is happy to find the estimated £100,000 or so needed to send a soldier to Afghanistan for a tour but the hassle of repairing any resultant psychological damage is deemed prohibitive.

Let the criminal justice system carry the fallout from war is the unspoken diktat. Shanks reportedly wanted help for his mental condition immediately after killing Vicki and while consumed with remorse. During his trial he apologised to her mother knowing it may have sounded hollow but he wanted her to know how much he adored her daughter. His words also offer an insight into the state of his mind, its torment over the things seen in war. 'I realise the implications of high velocity damage to a human body. I've seen it, I've treated it loads of times. I know what bombs and bullets do to a human being,' he said. Speak to the young men returning from Afghanistan and they say similar things. They too have learnt that a man can carry on living with part of his skull missing, how a scrap of molten shrapnel can slice a leg clean in two from fifty metres. What a roadside bomb does to a human. The smell of the dead; how some bodies keep their blood while others cannot wait to let it drain into the desert. They have learnt a man can continue towards his destination with his legs blown off. How, one afternoon, an Afghan army officer crawled on his stumps to safety. But their real fear is the IEDs, the hidden bombs that lace the land. One step and – bang – you've lost your leg or your best friend. Their randomness, their silent patience, exerts a terrible strain on those patrolling every day. The IEDs, mental health experts have observed, are capable of creating a profound guilt among those who survive. Why Frank? Why not me? Eventually the guilt will sour into rage.

Can a mind be mended? That depends on who you ask. Dr Jones believes it is possible, but accepts it requires a lot of work. The MoD adopts a more bullish approach, citing military psychiatrists on its website as saying that seven in ten sufferers will heal themselves within a month and that patients will 'nearly always be returned to full health'. Some believe it is a ludicrously over-optimistic assertion. Try, they say, telling that to those who still scream in the middle of night ten years after their last firefight, or the man whose scalp is smothered in scars not from shrapnel but self-harming or the teenager who carried the body of a dead pal and who wakes up leaning over his fiancée trying to lift her up, trying to save his friend's life.

Try telling Shanks and the thousands of others locked away that PTSD is just a passing phase, that it'll often clear itself up.

Although there is no denying that treatment for the condition has improved vastly since Shanks' deterioration, the consensus maintains it is nowhere near enough. Warnings from Combat Stress that the NHS cannot cope with military trauma have not prevented specialised psychiatric centres from closing down. Former servicemen have to rely on GPs and outpatients departments at NHS hospitals that are under-resourced and inexperienced in the specialist treatment required. Only a quarter of veterans even seem aware they are entitled to priority treatment on the NHS. Government plans for a state-funded PTSD treatment programme for veterans remain sketchy, say critics. Proposals for an early PTSD diagnosis programme have already been abandoned.

Cast alone on Civvy Street, ex-service personnel experience an acute sense of isolation that can compound psychological problems. They may have been in charge of millions of pounds of technology and capable of life and death judgements but in credit crunch Britain they are left scrabbling for jobs at the local supermarket. Inside the armed forces, colleagues are told to keep an eye out for sudden mood swings, but outside who's watching? Who was watching Shanks as he fell apart?

Like the war has changed the minds of those who fought in it, the conflicts of Afghanistan and Iraq in particular have altered Britain. Once enthusiastic men like Shanks return confused and embittered. Inside Britain an internal conflict emerges between those against the war, those who call veterans 'child killers' and the 'butchers of Basra', and those who joined up to serve their country just like their dads and granddads. The after-effects of Iraq and Afghanistan will be felt for decades. Shanks of course did not serve in either campaign but that is the point. It doesn't matter where and who. The wars of the future, like the past, will see Shanks' successors return from new wars. All over Helmand, at this very moment, in ditches and dusty corridors, his inheritors are patrolling a dangerous land. One day they will come home, the old self gone. Then the nightmares will build until they do something dreadful and are imprisoned for life. Or they might receive treatment.

Mark Townsend is an award-winning reporter and currently Home Affairs Editor of the Observer. *Born in Cumbria.*

Private Security Contractors in Iraq: the lifeline of neo-colonial rule

Haifa Zangana

Lest we forget

On Tuesday 9 October 2007, forty-nine-year-old Marou Awanis, an Iraqi mother of three, was driving her car, an old white Oldsmobile, in the Karrada district, in East Central Baghdad. Next to her sat thirty-year-old Genevia Jalal Antranick while two children were sitting in the back. Guards from a private security company opened fire killing Marou and Genevia. According to Ammar Falih, a shop owner who witnessed the scene, their faces were completely smashed. The hospital's report stated that they were shot in the head more than forty times.

The US embassy, in the Green Zone, issued a statement simply denying that Blackwater employees who work for them were involved in the 'incident'. The Australian-run Unity Resources Group (URG) employees claimed that Awanis came too close to a convoy they were protecting. Awanis was perceived as a threat. The eyewitnesses spoke otherwise. *The Guardian*'s record of those killed in Iraq, according to the US Logs on Wikileaks, has their entry as number 42379 with the time at 14:20 and the coordinates to the eighth decimal place, indicating the side of the street in Karrada. It has the term 'friendly fire' with two killed and two injured civilians.

Looking through the 'incident' lens raises questions, such as why did the two women venture into the dangerous streets of

Baghdad in October 2007, and how did they become a threat to the armed contractors of an Australian security firm in this residential area? This allows us to see the women as the Iraqi citizens they are in their own country occupied by foreign forces with their mercenaries. The answers would then help us see what is likely to happen in the coming years for Iraqis in relation to the occupiers and their neo-mercenaries, the private security contractors (PSCs).

Iraqi women coping with reality
Awanis was widowed in 2004, one year after the occupation, and became the sole head of the household responsible for supporting her three daughters.[1] She is one of a million Iraqi widows bringing up over five million orphans in a war zone, with almost no state welfare.

The Anglo-American occupation has deliberately dismantled the Iraqi state, the army, the police and the key structures of civil society. This has forced people back to the defences of their smaller communities with very limited resources, after thirteen years of the most brutal sanctions in modern times, often compared to the medieval siege of cities. At the start, the community defences helped at the local and neighbourhood level. However, the deliberately fostered sectarian and ethnic divisions of spoils amongst politicians and their warring militias became monstrous. One of the consequences is a major change in the public role of women which Awanis exemplifies. During the first three years of occupation women were mostly confined to their homes for their safety, protected by male relatives. But since men are the main target of US-led troops, and militias and death squads were supplied with long and varied lists of men's names, women had to step out to protect their homes, children and male relatives, and to carry on a semblance of normal life. A paradoxical situation prevailed in 2005-8 when women carried out most of the outdoor tasks, from getting food and fuel to searching for their loved ones in morgues and burying the dead. They relied on the fact that local militias are mostly made up of local youngsters still holding engrained values of respect and protection towards the aged, women and children regardless of their men folk. Women in 2007 were mostly collateral damage, not the direct object of violence from militias.

Furthermore, by mid-2007, one in eight Iraqis had become refugees, with up to 50,000 more people leaving their homes each month. UNHCR have said the exodus was the largest long-term population movement since the displacement of the Palestinians after the creation of Israel in 1948. The Iraqi Red Crescent estimates that two thirds of the displaced are women and children, often living in female-headed households.

Marou Awanis and her family stayed at home. To earn her living, she came up with an idea, based on the needs of women in her neighbourhood and others nearby, to run a taxi service to and from work and to accompany their children to and from school. The idea was welcomed by many women as a mode of survival and coping with the harsh reality and lawlessness in Iraq, especially allaying the fear of the kidnapping of children.

On the day of her killing, Awanis was simply taking Genevia from work and the two children from school. None of them knew about URG.

Other 'incidents'

The killing of the two women, and traumatising of the two children, was not the first criminal act by URG. The same firm[2] shot dead seventy-two-year-old Professor Qays Juma, in March 2006, as he approached an intersection being blockaded for a convoy URG was protecting. The firm claimed that he did not stop when he was ordered to. No one has been held responsible for the killing of the two women or the professor.

A massacre was to briefly highlight the role of the contractors in the media. On 16 September 2007, in al-Nisoor Square, Mansoor district, in West Central Baghdad, seventeen Iraqi civilians were killed and more than twenty wounded, including many women and children. The massacre – which was committed this time by employees of Blackwater, the Pentagon's security contractor, using firearms and a helicopter to shoot civilian bystanders – was described in a US statement as an 'incident'.

Iraqis know that these 'incidents' are the tip of the iceberg. There are more under-reported crimes which are committed either by private security contractors alone or together with occupation troops, since independent media reporting is extremely rare and Iraqi journalists have been targeted, beaten up, detained, or prohibited from approaching places where 'incidents' have occurred. In 2007, the Interior Ministry announced that journalists would be banned from the sites of explosions.[3] It is left to a few independent Iraqi NGOs, working under extremely dangerous circumstances and challenging the silence of the outside world, to record and document the killings in order not to forget, to have names of the victims imprinted in our collective memory, hoping for justice in the future. The 391,832 Wikileaks reports ('The Iraq War Logs'), which document the war and occupation in Iraq, from 1 January 2004 to 31 December 2009, proved that the US military has a record of many of these 'incidents' which could be used as evidence in the future.

By 2007, PSCs outnumbered US troops, providing an ever-widening range of services. The State Department says they employ them to protect US diplomats and officials in their running of the occupied country of thirty million people. The Pentagon says it employs them to protect their convoys of ammunition, equipment and supplies to the scores of military bases and hundreds of Forward Operating Stations across the eighteen provinces and various cities. With time the much wider remit of the PSCs became clear. They have roles in running prisons, interrogation, interpreting, officially training Iraqi forces and privately training local forces. They provide intelligence and combat role support with practically no limit in the use of vehicles, helicopters and technology.

Furthermore, women from Third World nations have been lured into sex traps after being promised well-paid jobs in Dubai. A former Blackwater guard said, in a written testimony, that he saw colleagues and American soldiers paying Iraqi girls, some as young as twelve and thirteen, for sex acts.[4]

Contrary to what the occupation and the media try to promote, the presence of 180,000 US-led multinational forces, 180,000 contractors and mercenaries,[5] has been the main problem in Iraq and not the 'inherent violence in Iraqis themselves'.

Together, the military and the contractors often took part in killing and wounding civilians in 'escalation-of-force' incidents, 'situations where occupation troops on patrol, manning checkpoints or escorting vehicle convoys have opened fire on men, women and children they considered a threat'.[6] Where, according to Senator Patrick Leahy, 'Whole families gunned down, or only young children left alive after their parents in the front seat were riddled with bullets.'[7] These incidents happened so often that many were not investigated.[8] Xe/Blackwater guards, alone, were found to have been involved in nearly 200 escalation–of–force incidents that involved the firing of shots since 2005.[9]

Withdrawal of occupation troops

In November 2008, under the Bush administration and Maliki's regime, two US–Iraq agreements were signed: the Status of the Forces Agreement (SOFA) and the long–term Strategic Framework Agreement.

SOFA deals with the issue of legal immunity for US troops and dates for a full withdrawal, while the Strategic Framework Agreement focuses on shaping future cooperation on fighting terrorism, counterinsurgency, political, cultural, and economic relations among many others.

The partial withdrawal of US troops on 1 September 2009 meant, in reality, moving from direct military occupation to neo–colonial rule, evoking similarities with the 1930 agreement to consolidate the British colonial rule of Iraq. According to General Raymond Odierno, US commander in Iraq 2008–2010, the US military presence for the time being can be summarised as follows: 50,000 US troops, 94 US bases, up to 65,000 contractors, along with 250,000 Iraqi army and over 500,000 Iraqi police. Furthermore, there will be three 'enduring presence posts', in addition to the US embassy, the biggest in the world. The reason behind the US presence is that, according to General Odierno, 'We're training, advising and assisting them. We continue to support our Provincial Reconstruction Teams and the UN for civil capacity, and we conduct partner counterterrorism operations.'[10]

PSCs continue to work together with US forces on all levels to provide convoy security teams, quick reaction forces and security for contracted vehicle recovery teams, as well as support for special operations units located throughout Iraq where boundaries between US forces and contractors are increasingly blurred. Details of who is to be counted in the PSCs in Iraq are not clear. One official US figure is of 11,610 PSC employees in Iraq, of which 581 (5%) provided unarmed services. This figure does not include contractors, armed or unarmed, who are training security forces, analysing intelligence, or conducting interrogations. PSC employees in Iraq include US and British nationals, some other thirty countries' nationals and Iraqis.[11]

Iraqis are cheaper to hire by PSCs. At the end of 2003, an Iraqi interpreter working for the US military was paid $5 daily compared with $200 for a foreign employee (mostly from other Arab countries or US citizens of Arab origin). By 2009, salaries of US interpreters had risen to between $108,750 and $175,500, putting them in the top 6% for personal income in the United States, while Iraqi interpreters' salaries are $13,200 to $15,600 a year.[12]

There are advantages for using Iraqis as security contractors, such as knowing the language and areas and buying loyalty through providing jobs and benefits. The problem is that Iraqis, in general, are not to be trusted by the occupation, for fear of the resistance's infiltration, no matter how keen some Iraqis are to collaborate, whether through conviction, naivety or economic need.

There are contradictory reports about the number of registered PSCs. According to the Iraqi Ministry of Interior, 'there are currently 82 PSCs registered and licensed (56 Iraqi companies and 26 foreign companies). These PSCs are employing more than 30,000 armed employees working for a variety of government and private sector clients.'[13] 'Iraqi' companies are not necessarily owned by Iraqis or employing Iraqis only but could simply be registered under the patronage of one Iraqi official or other.

Since PSCs are a huge source of income and corruption is integrated within their structure and function, billions of dollars from the public budget are spent on what is called security for officials, a euphemism for largesse for the new elite.

Over 44 per cent of the Iraqi government budget is spent on security in various forms across the ministries. Let us look at some numbers to understand this staggering proportion of the budget: there are 325 MPs, 42 cabinet ministers, numerous Iraqi advisors, and hundreds of US and British advisors. Each one of them has on average 30–40 armed security guards. MPs have allocated funds for 30 guards each for themselves, the ministers for 40 guards each, and advisors for numbers according to their rank. We can talk of a few thousand officials, elected or otherwise, in all the eighteen Iraqi provinces that rely for their personal and home protection on security guards paid for by public funds. If you add in the armed guards of the office buildings and facilities, we can imagine the number of these semi-official armed individuals (often, they are members of the militias which comprise the backbone of the political parties) to be equal to the official number of the new Iraqi army and police force, totalling 750,000. Thus we have one officially armed security person with impunity for every five Iraqi households – a profitable recipe for enslaving people using their own wealth. Add to that their arms, equipment, vehicles, and quarters, to see how lucrative is the Iraqi branch of the international private security business.

Furthermore, there have been multi-million-dollar contracts to sell Iraq all sort of obsolete arms and fraudulent technologies. Some are intended to expand the use of biometrics like iris scans, fingerprints, DNA and other traditional, as well as novel, crime lab tools and remote sensing devices. A current example is a contract with a British firm called ATSC (UK) Ltd to supply small hand-held wands, used to detect explosives in cars at checkpoints. The Ministry of the Interior bought an unspecified large quantity for $85 million at a cost of up to $60,000 apiece, when the wands could be purchased for $18,500. The irony is that the wands were found to be absolutely useless, but continue to be used in Iraq.

Iraqi reports
In general, PSCs are seen as the new mercenaries and as part and parcel of the occupation and its neo-colonial rule. In fact, their profitable business based on the continuity of war and occupation, their immunity from local laws and the heavy reliance of the US military on them have helped make them, not, as they used to be, a mere extension, but the lifeline of imperial expansion to consolidate its powers.

Accordingly, their crimes have been extended far beyond shootings and killings. Jose L. Gomez del Prado, Executive President of the UN Working Group on the Use of Mercenaries, reported recently: 'In the course of our research, since 2006, we have collected ample information which indicates the negative impact of the activities of "private contractors", "private soldiers" or "guns for hire", whatever denomination we may choose to name the individuals who are employed by private military and security companies as civilians but are also generally heavily armed. In the cluster of human rights violations allegedly perpetrated by employees of the companies the Working Group has examined, one can find: summary executions, acts of torture, cases of arbitrary detention, trafficking of persons and serious health damages caused by PMSC employee activities, as well as attempts against the right of self-determination.'[14]

Various independent Iraqi organisations have consistently reported that car bombs in markets and crowded places near mosques and waves of killings are coordinated.[15] They normally follow successful attacks of the Iraqi resistance against occupation forces, and are orchestrated by shadowy occupation-funded groups linked to 'security advisors', who implement counterinsurgency tactics like those we saw in Vietnam, El Salvador and Northern Ireland.

It is worth noting that, despite the usual playing down of the crimes committed by PSCs, some Iraqi officials are hinting at their responsibility, although without holding them legally accountable. Major General Mohammed Nei'ma, chief of operations at the Ministry of Interior, said, 'There are more than 200 foreign and Iraqi security companies unauthorized by us and a large number of these companies are involved in terrorist acts.'[16]

A recent statement by the Ministry of Interior revealed that twelve non-registered PSCs, in Karrada district in Baghdad, were found to be involved in the kidnapping and killing of civilians. Baghdad Operations Command has noted that the assailants in a majority of armed attacks in Baghdad were wearing uniforms of PSCs.[17]

The reality on the ground, with the partial withdrawal of US forces and mushrooming of various US–third country– Iraqi PSCs, marks the initial phase of the neo-colonial rule under the long-term US–Iraq Strategic Framework Agreement. This usurps Iraq's sovereignty while breeding a new class of corrupt politicians, increasingly powerful militias, and co-opted businessmen and technocrats.

To put an end to the presence of PSCs in Iraq, it is vital to cut off its umbilical cord, namely the occupation army, with its advisors and consultants. No peace is conceivable in Iraq without the full withdrawal of foreign troops and ending all plans for military bases. The next step is to implement long-forgotten international law, to include the banning of PSCs and the prosecution of those who are guilty of killings, corruption, human rights abuses and torture.

Haifa Zangana is an Iraqi author and activist. She has published three novels and four collections of short stories. She is a founding member of the International Association of Contemporary Iraqi Studies (IACIS), and co-founder of Women Solidarity for an Independent and Unified Iraq. She was an advisor for the UNDP report 'Towards the rise of women in the Arab world' in 2005. She writes a weekly column for Al Quds Al Arabi, contributes to British and US papers and lectures regularly on Iraqi literature and women's issues.

Footnotes

[1] Iraq – Killing of Mary Awanis – 13 min 25 sec documentary by Sophie McNeill [21 November 2007] http://www.journeyman.tv/57746/short-films/killing-of-mary-awanis.html

[2] URG, an Australian private military and security company, uses a number of ex-military Chileans to provide security to the Australian Embassy in Baghdad. ABC News, reported by *La Tercera*, Chile, 16 September, 2010.

[3] Mohamed Abdel Dayem, CPJ's Middle East and North Africa programme coordinator says; 'But bombs are not the only factor obstructing news coverage. We call on security forces to stop preventing journalists from covering the aftermath of such attacks – we ask them to let journalists do their job.' In Iraq, bomb kills one journalist; another denied access, CPJ, 15 December 2010.

[4] Despite Allegations, No Prosecutions for War Zone Sex Trafficking, Nick Schwellenbach and Carol D. Leonnig, Center for Public Integrity, 26 July 2010.

[5] The numbers include at least 21,000 Americans, 43,000 foreign contractors and about 118,000 Iraqis. Private security contractors, who are hired to protect government officials and buildings, were not fully counted in the survey, according to industry and government officials. See Private Contractors Outnumber US Troops in Iraq, T. Christian Miller, *The Los Angeles Times*, 4 July 2007.

[6] Pentagon: U.S. troops shot 429 Iraqi civilians at checkpoints, Nancy A. Youssef, McClatchy Newspapers, 11 July 2007.

[7] Statement Of Sen. Patrick Leahy, Preventing Civilian Casualties In Iraq, 29 September 2006.

[8] Lieutenant Jonathan Morgenstein, an officer attached in 2004–2005 to a marine civil affairs unit – which investigated 'escalation of force' incidents – told *The Nation*: 'You physically could not do an investigation every time a civilian was wounded or killed because it just happens a lot and you'd spend all your time doing that.'

[9] Beyond WikiLeaks: The Privatization of War, Jose L. Gomez del Prado, t r u t h o u t, 26 December 2010.

[10] Department Of Defence (DOD) News Briefing with Gen. Odierno from the Pentagon, 4 June 2010.
http://www.defense.gov/transcripts/transcript.aspx?transcriptid=4632

[11] As of March 2010, according to the DOD. See 'CRS Report for Congress, The Department of Defense's Use of Private Security Contractors in Iraq and Afghanistan: Background, Analysis, and Options for Congress', Moshe Schwartz, 22 June 2010.

[12] GLS interpreters in Iraq threaten to strike over pay cuts, James Warden, *Stars and Stripes*, 2 February 2009.

[13] 'CRS Report for Congress, The Department of Defense's Use of Private Security Contractors in Iraq and Afghanistan: Background, Analysis, and Options for Congress', Moshe Schwartz, 22 June 2010.

[14] Beyond WikiLeaks: The Privatization of War, Jose L. Gomez del Prado, t r u t h o u t, 26 December 2010.

[15] Iraqi Rabita reports eyewitness accounts, see www.iraqirabita.org, also Robert Fisk: Seen through a Syrian lens, 'unknown Americans' are provoking civil war in Iraq, *The Independent,* 28 April 2006. For the relationship between the occupation and death squads see Max Fuller, 'Crying Wolf: Media Disinformation and Death Squads in Occupied Iraq', Global Research, 10 November 2005.

[16] 'Armies of private security guards of thirty-six foreign security companies officially registered and more than two hundred companies operating in Iraq are unauthorised', Mou'ad Fayadh, Asharq Al Awsat, 1 December 2006. (In Arabic)

[17] UR News, 8 December 2010 (In Arabic):
http://www.uragency.net/index.php?aa=news&id22=14639

Justice for Iraq
Mike Phipps

Today the two most common reactions to the invasion and occupation of Iraq within the political establishment are self-justification and amnesia. For many in the first category, the 2010 elections in Iraq – described as credible and plausible, rather than fair or free – made the entire invasion and occupation worthwhile. They brought a sense of closure to a necessary, if painful, process.

'Former President Bush's gut instincts that this region craved democracy were always right,' wrote Thomas Friedman of the *New York Times* at the time of the 2010 elections, in a piece entitled 'It's up to the Iraqis now. Good luck.' You would think the last troops had already left, but in fact 50,000 US military were due to remain until the end of 2011 – and possibly longer if either the Iraqi or US government request it.

This search for good news where there is little is not new. The 2005 elections, which entrenched sectarian divisions and institutionalised corruption and abuse, were also hailed at the time by President George Bush and Prime Minister Tony Blair as a justification for what they had done to Iraq. After the 2010 poll, it took several months and several visits from the US Vice President and State Department officials to cobble together a government. Nobody expected it to do much to improve anything.

In November 2010, the Iraqi parliament was told the country had run out of money to pay for widows' benefits, farm crops and other programmes for the poor. When a government finally did emerge, one politician claimed that Cabinet seats had been bought at a secret meeting in the house of an Iraqi businessman.

The confidence of those who continue to justify the occupation took a further dent in November 2010 with the publication of leaked documentation on the Wikileaks website. Hundreds of incidents of abuse and torture of prisoners by Iraqi security services, up to and including rape and murder, were documented. US forces are alleged to have colluded in these activities, as well as themselves continuing to abuse prisoners long after the Abu Ghraib scandal broke in 2004. US forces operating helicopter gunships were also accused of killing fourteen unarmed civilians in a series of previously unreported incidents.

The Independent's Robert Fisk observed, 'If this vast treasury of secret reports had proved that the body count was much lower than trumpeted by the press, that US soldiers never tolerated Iraqi police torture, rarely shot civilians at checkpoints and always brought killer mercenaries to account, US generals would be handing these files out to journalists free of charge on the steps of the Pentagon. They are furious not because secrecy has been breached, or because blood may be spilt, but because they have been caught out telling the lies we always knew they told.'

British troops were also deeply implicated. *The Guardian* reported that 90 complaints involving 128 Iraqi civilians were being investigated in the aftermath of the Wikileaks revelations. In the same week, they discovered that the British military had been training interrogators in techniques that include threats, sensory deprivation and enforced nakedness in an apparent breach of the Geneva conventions.

Small wonder that those who can no longer defend the occupation of Iraq would prefer to forget the whole thing. It's time to move on, draw a line, admit we made a mistake and so on. This appears to be the thinking of the new leadership of the Labour Party, among others.

'Moving on' is not so easy for Iraqis. They are still living with the catastrophic effects of the invasion. One in two households in Baghdad alone have lost a family member. A million have died. A further million have been left disabled. One in six Iraqis is an orphan. An estimated sixteen per cent of the Iraqi population has been uprooted. Drinking water remains unsafe. Basic foods and necessities are increasingly beyond the reach of ordinary Iraqis, thanks to soaring inflation unleashed by the occupation's free market ideology. Unemployment is regularly estimated at over fifty per cent. Seventy per cent of doctors are estimated to have fled the country. Homelessness is widespread. Water shortages are destroying agriculture, power shortages crippling industry. Permanent damage has been inflicted on the country's historic cultural heritage.

As Patrick Cockburn wrote for *The Independent* in July 2010, 'American troops leave behind a country that is a barely floating wreck. Baghdad feels like a city under military occupation, with horrendous traffic jams caused by the 1,500 checkpoints and streets blocked off by miles of concrete blast walls that strangle communications within the city. Baghdad remains one of the most dangerous cities in the world, riskier to walk around than Kabul or Kandahar... Violence may be down, but few of the two million Iraqi refugees in Jordan and Syria think it safe enough to go home. A further one and half million people are Internally Displaced Persons, forced out of their homes by sectarian pogroms in 2006 and 2007 and too frightened to return. Of these, some half a million people try to survive in squatter camps which Refugees International describes as lacking "basic services, including water, sanitation and electricity, and built on precarious places – under bridges, alongside railroad tracks and amongst garbage dumps".'

To that can be added a culture of embezzlement that can be traced to the deliberate overpricing of contracts by multinational corporations in the first days of the occupation. In 2010, the country was ranked the fourth most corrupt in the entire world.

Iraq is also becoming increasingly authoritarian. Brutality and torture are rife in its jails. In September 2010, Amnesty International reported that up to 30,000 prisoners, including many veterans of the US detention system, remain detained without rights in Iraq and are frequently tortured, or abused. They assessed the human rights situation as dire, with arbitrary arrests and secret detention common.

Additionally, new laws have been passed to crack down on the independent media.

'The current climate of terror and impunity has seen an increase in violence against journalists by members of the Iraqi security forces,' Reporters Without Borders said in 2010.

Human Rights Watch have called on Iraqi authorities to stop blocking peaceful demonstrations and arresting and intimidating organisers. Iraqi security forces cracked down on demonstrations against the lack of government services in the summer of 2010, refusing numerous requests for public demonstrations, arresting organisers and using violent police tactics which caused deaths and injuries.

The position of trade unions has also deteriorated significantly in Iraq. In 2010, the police raided and shut down trade union offices using legislation from the Saddam Hussein era. There are reports too of police crackdowns on gay people. The Education Ministry has banned theatre and music classes. Many girls still dare not go to school or college because of violence and kidnappings.

Iraqi society has been traumatised by the experience of occupation. As Naomi Klein argued in her book *The Shock Doctrine*, the opening US military bombardment provided the social and psychological disorientation necessary to launch a crippling economic policy, including mass privatisation, free trade and flat taxes. To ensure these policies took hold, local elections were overturned in favour of occupation-appointed puppets. Opponents of these 'freedoms' were repressed as Saddamists or Al-Qaeda.

When elections were first held, occupation forces organised them on the basis of Shia and Sunni slates. What better way to foster sectarian divisions where few existed before, given that victory meant jobs, favours and kickbacks for the group in power. Thenceforth, religious affiliation could be a deciding factor in whether you worked or had state protection, and thus became a significant source of friction. But, conveniently, it did allow the occupiers to reinvent their role as that of arbitrator between warring religious factions.

The consequences of this policy continue to reverberate. Towards the end of 2010, thousands of Christians fled Iraq, following attacks on their communities, with houses and churches bombed in Baghdad and Mosul in particular.

Some of the long-term effects of the occupation are most felt in the city of Fallujah. US forces flattened three-quarters of the city in their 2004 bombardment, with up to 6,000 people killed. Some 36,000 of the city's 50,000 homes were destroyed, along with 60 schools and 65 mosques and shrines. Up to 200,000 residents were forced to flee.

The US admits that it used white phosphorous as a battlefield weapon in its assault on Fallujah. Its effects are similar to that of napalm, burning bodies to the bone, as documentary evidence in the city has confirmed. And on 30 December 2010, *The Guardian* reported, 'A study examining the causes of a dramatic spike in birth defects in the Iraqi city of Fallujah has for the first time concluded that genetic damage could have been caused by weaponry used in US assaults that took place six years ago.'

One suspected cause of the birth defects is depleted uranium shells, fired in 2004 by US forces in the city, which contain ionising radiation. A recent survey in the city showed a four-fold increase in all cancers and a twelve-fold increase in childhood cancer in under-fourteen-year olds.

The UK also used depleted uranium weapons during the invasion. 'UK forces used about 1.9 metric tons of depleted uranium ammunition in the Iraq war in 2003,' Defence Secretary Liam Fox has admitted.

Those British forces may have now withdrawn, but the foreign occupation of Iraq is far from over. Despite President Obama's election promise to withdraw US forces, the actual agreements don't exactly say this.

In June 2009, Foreign Policy in Focus underlined the discrepancy between appearance and reality: 'The United States is looking to withdraw from Iraq in name only, as it appears that up to 50,000 military personnel will remain after the deadline.' It continued, 'Instead of sending soldiers stationed in cities home, the military has been expanding and building new bases in rural areas to accommodate soldiers affected by the June 30th deadline. And Congress just passed a war-spending bill that includes more funding for military construction inside Iraq.' Additionally, the US State Department asked Congress in 2010 to approve funds to more than double the number of private security contractors in Iraq.

In September 2010, the Iraqi Defence Minister said that some form of US military presence would be needed at least until 2016 for training, support and maintenance purposes, as well as help with intelligence gathering.

Obama's administration renamed its activities in the country 'Operation New Dawn'. In a typical smoke and mirrors exercise, combat units were renamed advisory units, while continuing the same frontline duties. Thus, while the combat mission formally ended on 31 August 2010, AP reported a month later that, 'American troops found themselves battling heavily armed militants assaulting an Iraqi military headquarters in the centre of Baghdad. The fighting killed twelve people and wounded dozens.'

The same month a joint US-Iraqi attack on Fallujah was reported to have killed at least ten civilians and injured many others. Despite the supposed advisory role that US troops were now supposed to be playing, helicopter gunships were deployed. Two months later US troops shot and killed an Iraqi engineer at Baghdad Airport who failed to respond to hand signals to pull over. And in December 2010, US fighter jets reportedly pounded a region in Iraq's central governorate of Babil. Despite all the hype about withdrawal, a US military spokesman said, 'Our rules of engagement have not changed.'

'Since the Americans have declared the end of combat operations,' Foreign Policy reported in September 2010, 'US Stryker and MRAP vehicles can be seen conducting patrols without Iraqi escorts in parts of the country and the Americans continue to conduct unilateral military operations in Mosul and elsewhere, even if under the guise of "force protection" or "countering improvised explosive devices".'

On every level, Iraq is still being held back from full independence. Until they were lifted at the start of 2011, the UN's sanctions forced Iraq to pay five per cent of its oil revenues in reparations, mostly to Kuwait. Elections have been conducted under occupation and the country's economic wealth sold off under occupation.

In 2007, the Transnational Foundation for Peace and Future Research, whose board member Hans von Sponeck was formerly UN Humanitarian Coordinator, issued an important paper on the future of Iraq, observing: 'The invasion and ongoing occupation is a political, intellectual and moral disaster. A withdrawal that leaves Iraq at its own fate without any war reparations, aid, opportunities for socio-political healing, etc. would be yet another.'

There are several issues that still need to be addressed. What should happen to the tens of thousands of Iraqis, including children, still detained with no prospect of legal process? Who will clean up the cluster bombs and depleted uranium warheads, which in heavily bombarded areas such as Fallujah have wrought such havoc with people's health? How can Iraq extricate itself from oil extraction contracts signed away by its puppet government and return to full sovereignty over its economic affairs? What can be done to heal the trauma whose long-term effects distort the development of all post-conflict societies, often violently? What kind of financial compensation should the perpetrators pay for their illegal and immoral occupation?

In 2008, a London conference organised by Iraq Occupation Focus and attended by a wide range of activists, many of them Iraqis, issued the following declaration:

'We call on those states responsible for the invasion and occupation of Iraq to terminate their illegal and immoral war, and express our solidarity with the Iraqi people in their struggle for peace, justice and self-determination. In particular, we demand:

· An immediate end to the US- and UK-led occupation of Iraq;

· Urgent action to fully address the current humanitarian crises facing Iraq's people, including help for the more than three million refugees and displaced persons;

· An end to all foreign interference in Iraq's affairs, including its oil industry, so that Iraqis can exercise their right to self-determination;

· Compensation and reparations from those countries responsible for war and sanctions on Iraq;

· Prosecution of all those responsible for war crimes, human rights abuses, and the theft of Iraq's resources.

We demand justice for Iraq.

None of these issues have been addressed. The US military occupation continues, despite President Obama's campaign promises. Far from helping alleviate Iraq's humanitarian crisis, the British government is currently forcibly deporting Iraqi refugees back to that country. Iraq's oil wealth has been handed over in long-term contracts at knock-down prices to multinational companies. Not a penny of compensation has been offered for the war itself, although paltry sums have been paid to families after Western troops killed individual Iraqis. And far from being brought to account, the perpetrators are making a fortune from their activities.

In December 2010, the *London Evening Standard* reported that a company set up by former Prime Minister Tony Blair has been paid more than £27 million for advice to Kuwait. He is accused of cashing in on his decision to take Britain into Iraq in 2003.

Other leading politicians have also done well, such as Malcolm Rifkind, former Foreign Secretary and Conservative MP for Kensington, who headed ArmorGroup, until its recent takeover, which has made millions providing mercenary contractors in Iraq.

The occupation has been profitable too for Group 4 Security, which took over ArmorGroup and provides the British Army with security in southern Iraq. In 2009, former Home Secretary John Reid was hired as an advisor to this company, at a salary of £50,000 a year. Another British beneficiary is De La Rue, which got the $120 million contract to print Iraq's new currency, paid for by Iraq's oil revenues. It was printed in Basingstoke and flown in on twenty-seven specially chartered flights – the Iraqi Government had no control over the process. Sir Jeremy Greenstock, the deputy 'viceroy' in Iraq in the first two years of the occupation, is on the board.

Business as usual, for some, it would seem. But this stands in marked contrast to the public opposition to the war when it began – and the sense of anger still felt by an astonishing forty per cent of people in the UK, according to a 2010 poll. Clearly, the novelist Sue Townsend, writing in *The Guardian* in 2010, expressed the feelings of many, when she 'wept tears of shame, rage, and pity as British and American planes dropped their "strategic" bombs over Baghdad. I wondered if Blair was sitting on a sofa with his family watching shock and awe… could he look his children in the eye when the transmission was over? I have never recovered from the shock of that night. I have been told my fixation with Blair and his involvement with the invasion of Iraq is unhealthy – "that was all back in the day, get over it, move forward." But I can't.'

Neither can thousands of others who want to see Tony Blair held to account and even tried for war crimes. This is why they go out and picket him every time he appears in public, at a book signing or to make a speech.

Many years ago, Martin Luther King declared that peace is not the absence of conflict, but the presence of justice. Eight years after our government started an immoral and arguably illegal war, based on lies and deceit, is it not about time that the people of Iraq got some elementary justice after all the killing and destruction?

For more information, see justiceforiraq.blogspot.com or visit http://lists.riseup.net/www/info/iraqfocus to subscribe to the fortnightly email newsletter of Iraq Occupation Focus, an organisation set up to campaign to end the occupation of Iraq, provide practical solidarity for Iraqis and disseminate information in Britain about the realities of the occupation.

Mike Phipps is a founder member of Iraq Occupation Focus and joint editor of its fortnightly electronic newsletter.

Route Irish Production Notes

Ken Loach
Rebecca O'Brien
Mark Womack
Andrea Lowe

Ken Loach

Director

The challenge is always to find the microcosm that suggests the bigger picture: the unresolved conflict, the contradiction that, when explored, reveals the landscape.

Rebecca O'Brien

Producer

After *Looking For Eric* we felt it was important to make something serious and uncompromising and our French partners on that film, Pascal Caucheteux at Why Not and Vincent Maraval at Wild Bunch, were willing to support us fully. It was excellent to be able to work with them again, the financing became simple and straightforward and it gave me the opportunity to concentrate on the production. Our other regular European partners came on board along with North West Vision in the UK.

We filmed in Jordan for the Iraq scenes – not only did the Royal Jordanian Film Commission prove very supportive in setting up the production but there are many Iraqi refugees there who were able to work with us as supporting cast. Their truly harrowing stories brought the truth of what we were filming into close perspective. It was a joy to work in Liverpool again – it's a really manageable city full of wily characters and charm.

Mark Womack

Fergus

Ken has you do a lot of research. He'll have you meet a lot of people that might be similar to the character. You have a lot of conversations that might be useful and read a lot about the world the character lives in, so when the scenes are thrown at you, you've met contractors and heard all their stories and you can build the character from that. You also spend a lot of time with the characters you're going to work with and you bond with them. I went to army boot camp with John Bishop who plays Frankie and Trevor who plays Nelson, so I got to know them quite well. We were already comfortable with each other by the time it came to filming. I was upset on the first day to be told John was dead, I felt pretty much how I imagine it feels to lose a friend. John was great because he knew all along and he kept it quiet.

Fergus is on a path of self-destruction like many of the soldiers I met with combat stress. One of the guys I met said you go in the army and they turn you on, but nobody turns you off. How can you go from seeing what you've seen in Iraq and Afghanistan to shopping in Sainsbury's with the wife and kids? Some guys can adjust, but a lot of them can't.

Andrea Lowe

Rachel

I'd seen most of Ken's films and I thought, like a lot of people perhaps, that they are improvisation based. But they're not, there's a beautiful script. Where the improvisation comes in is in the development of the character.

Sometimes you know parts of the script that the other actors don't, but you don't ask them and they wouldn't tell you because we all really enjoy the process. It ensures that your reactions are natural and keeps things fresh and spontaneous and so as an actor you don't overanalyse. The essence of Ken's films is the truth in people and this film is about broken people.

When we were working on the backstory we established that Rachel had met Fergus first and she's had a bit of a wild past and been into the music scene and travelled around a lot, she's just decided to become a personal trainer and she's into her yoga and they met in a gym. He's dark and moody and she would perhaps have gone for it with him in the past, but she's at a time in her life when that's not what she wants, so there's an unfulfilled attraction between them. Fergus introduces her to Frankie and she falls for him, he's big and light and fun. After Frankie dies, Fergus is in a dark place and can't let her in to save him. They can't rescue each other, it's tragic.

Film Credits

Fergus	Mark Womack
Rachel	Andrea Lowe
Frankie	John Bishop
Walker	Geoff Bell
Haynes	Jack Fortune
Harim	Talib Rasool
Craig	Craig Lundberg
Nelson	Trevor Williams
Tommy	Russell Anderson
Jamie	Jamie Michie
Young Fergus	Bradley Thompson
Young Frankie	Daniel Foy
Marisol	Najwa Nimri
Frankie's Mother	Maggie Southers
David	R David
Andy	Anthony Schumacher
Undertaker	Gary Cargill
Peggy	Donna Elson
Steve	Stephen Lord
Jay	Jaimes Locke

and Natalie Flood, Andy Dwyer, Taban Othman,
Ali Karami, Nasredine Banda, Nick Baty

Yousef	Tayf Basil
Ranj	Ranj Hawra
Mother	Hind Kamil

and Malik Amir, Mohsen Fakhir, Aseel Salam, Kevin Burton,
Tagreed Asad, Omar Abdelaazeez and Sajida Hassan

Director	Ken Loach
Screenplay	Paul Laverty
Producer	Rebecca O'Brien
Executive Producers	Pascal Caucheteux
	Vincent Maraval
Production Designer	Fergus Clegg
Photography	Chris Menges
Recordist	Ray Beckett
Casting	Kahleen Crawford
Costume Designer	Sarah Ryan
Assistant Directors	David Gilchrist
	Michael Queen

Locations	Claire Newton
Sound Editor	Kevin Brazier
Line Producer	Tim Cole
Editor	Jonathan Morris
Music	George Fenton
Stunt Co-ordinator	Paul Heasman
Stunt Performers	Kid Richmond
	Barrett Snow
	Lee Sheward
	Gordon Seed
Production Co-ordinator	Eimhear McMahon
Production	Loren McLaughlan
	Sophie Agnew
	Owen Arnold
	Danny Boocock
Casting Assistant	Caroline Stewart
Research	Ann Cattrall
3rd Assistant Director	Julie Heskin
Unit Manager	Mark Volante
Runner	Chris Cavanagh
Drivers	Keith Wignall
	Paul Walker
Focus Puller	Carl Hudson
Clapper Loaders	Amaury Duquenne
	Joachim Philippe
Camera Trainee	Ricky Mears
Additional Camera	Jason Bulley
Script Consultant	Roger Smith
Script Supervisor	Susanna Lenton
Stills Photographer	Joss Barratt
Gaffer	Lee Walters
Best Boy	Paul Sharp
Electricians	Laurent Van Eijs
	Adam Walker
Boom Operator	Pete Murphy
Sound Assistant	Ric Perrin
Playback Technicians	Rick Bailey
	Ben Hodkinson
	Red Frog
Art Director	Grant Armstrong
Assistant Art Director	Julie Ann Horan

Prop Buyer	Anita Gupta
Prop Master	Colin Mutch
Dressing Props	Mark Reynolds
Standby Props	Ben Johnson
Armourers	Steve Wilkerson
Weapons Co-ordinator	Charlie Phillips
	Perdix Firearms
Action Vehicle Co-ordinator	Neil Adams
SFX Supervisor	David Harris
SFX Senior Technician	Stuart Wishart
Construction Manager	Danny Sumsion
Carpenters	Alex Robertson
	Colin Relph
Standby Carpenter	Mark Brady
Stagehand	Johnny Mellor
Painters	Paul Curren
	Martin Feely
Make-up and Hair Designer	Carli Mather
Costume Supervisor	Sam Scragg
Dailies	Michael Biggam
	Mark Garside
	Lynn Gibson
	Kay McIntosh
	Victoria Yates
	Chris Wanklyn
	Mark Jones
	Paul Taylor
	Mark Burness
	Antoine Doyen
Production Accountant	Tina Shadick
Assistant Accountants	Marc Grant
	Habib Rahman
Auditor	Malde & Company
1st Assistant Editor	Anthony Morris
2nd Assistant Editor	Paul Clegg
Sound Transfers	Steve Carr
Effects Editor / Foley Recordist	Robert Brazier
Dialogue / Foley Editor	Ben Brazier
Foley Artists	Rowena Wilkinson
	Sue Harding
Re-recording Mixers	Ian Tapp
	James Doyle

Sound Mix Technician	Tim Siddall
Paramedics	Mediprop
Caterers	Michael Ross
	Red Chutney
Security	Keith Jenkins
	Tony Molloy
Travel Agents	Katie Grist,
	Alhambra Travel

JORDAN UNIT

Production Services Supervisor	Linda Mutawi
	The Royal Film
	Commission
Production Services Company	International Traders
Production Manager	Fuad Khalil
Production Co-ordinator	Reem Bandak
Production Assistant	Ashraf Mezied
Production Accountant	Maha Hanna
Assistant Location Manager	Saeb Abu Al Ragheb
3rd Assistant Director	Omar Sawalha
Runner	Arifa Bseiso
Best Boy	Jalal Khreisat
Third Man	Maggie Kabariti
Casting	Lara Atalla
	Raya Hamdan
	Basil Karim
Art Department	Karim Kheir
	Nasser Zoubi
Construction	Samy Keilani
	Samir Zeidan
	Ashraf Ahmed Alnawai
Wardrobe	Phaedra Dahdaleh
	Abdel Rayyan
Assistant Make-up	Reem Naber
Transportation	Omar Ayesh
	Omar Deeb (Abu Alaa)
	Nader Ayoub
	Jihad Tamimi
	Ahmad Smadi
	Majdi Abdul Qader
	Ziad Qariyouti
Vehicle Coordinator	Garo Youmdjian

Caterers	Wael Jabaji
Locations Security	Abu Rashed
First Aid Services	Civil Defence 19
Music Recorded by	Steve Price at Angel Recording Studios
Pro Tools	Mat Bartram
Programmer	Leigh Lawson

Music published by Shogun Music Ltd

Songs
'Rocks' performed by Primal Scream
Licensed courtesy of Sony Music Entertainment UK Ltd.
Words and music by
Bobby Gillespie, Robert Young & Andrew Innes © 1993
Published by EMI Music Publishing Limited & Complete Music Ltd.

'Baghdad' performed by Talib Rasool
Composed and Arranged by Ilham al-Madfai, Lyrics by Nizar Qabbani
Licensed courtesy of EMI Music Publishing Arabia.

Archive provided courtesy of
Journeyman Pictures, ITN Source, AlJazeera.

With thanks to:
The Veterans Mental Health Charity, Combat Stress; Rose Gentle, Deely
Cumming, Ruth Tanner & Paul Collins, War on Want; Simon Brown,
Tommy Moffat, Ryan Moffat, Ben Shaw, Clive Fairweather, Phil Shiner,
Grant Dalziel, Stephen Armstrong, Mazin Younis, Dr Neil Greenberg,
Cliff Holland, Patrick Cockburn, Tony Nelson, Dave Cotterill, Terence
Millar, Darren Adam; Julia Ravenscroft, Refugee Action; Maggi Green,
Ewan Roberts & Ben Kamara, Asylum Link Merseyside; Hannah Ward,
Refugee Council; Mark Townsend and to those many people who helped
but did not want to give their names.

George David & The Royal Film Commission – Jordan; Lynn Saunders
& Kevin Bell, Liverpool Film Office; Neil Scales, Mersey Ferries; Royal
Daffodil Captains Steve Atkinson & Peter Carroll; Steve Reading, Steve
Johnson, Karl Carberry, Staff at LA Productions, Staff at the Hope Street
Hotel, Staff at the Casa Club, the Officers and Sergeants of The Army
Training Regiment, Winchester; Stuart Griffiths, Massimo Mazzucco,
Mark Stucke and Tess the three-legged dog

Sixteen Films
Why Not Productions
Wild Bunch
Les Films de Fleuve, Urania Pictures, Tornasol Films,
Alta Producción & France 2 Cinéma
and
Canal +, France Télévisions, Cinécinéma, Sofica UGC 1,
Diaphana Distribution, Cinéart,
Canto Bros Productions & Vision+Media

A British/French/Italian/Belgian/Spanish Co-Production
Filmed on location in Liverpool and Jordan
Developed with the support of the MEDIA development fund.

Looking For Eric

Written by Paul Laverty, Directed by Ken Loach
ISBN: 978-1901927-41-2

Eric the postman is slipping through his own fingers... His chaotic family, his wild stepsons, and the cement mixer in the front garden don't help, but it is Eric's own secret that drives him to the brink. Can he face Lily, the woman he once loved thirty years ago? Despite outrageous efforts and misplaced goodwill from his football fan mates, Eric continues to sink.

In desperate times it takes a spliff and a special friend from foreign parts to challenge a lost postman to make that journey into the most perilous territory of all – the past. As the Chinese, and one Frenchman, say, 'He who is afraid to throw the dice, will never throw a six.'

Features the full screenplay, including extra scenes, sixteen pages of colour photographs, plus introductions from Paul Laverty, Ken Loach, Eric Cantona and production notes from the cast and crew.

Even the Rain

Written by Paul Laverty, Directed by Icíar Bollaín
ISBN: 978-1907862-05-2

Costa and Sebastian arrive in Cochabamba, Bolivia, to shoot a period film about Columbus's arrival in the Americas. Sebastian wants to upturn the entire conservative myth of Western Civilisation's arrival in the Americas as a force for good. Rather, his story is about what Columbus set in motion; the obsession with gold, the hunt for slaves by Spanish mastiffs, and punitive violence to those Indians who fought back. Costa just wants to get the film made on time and within budget. The battle to get their film made intertwines with the fight of their Bolivian crew members, deprived of their most basic rights, prohibited from collecting even the rain.

As Sebastian and Costa struggle with their film, the violence in the community in which they shoot increases by the day until the entire city explodes into the now infamous Bolivian Water War. Five hundred years after Columbus, sticks and stones confront the steel and gun powder of a modern army. David against Goliath once again. Only this time they fight not about gold, but the simplest of life-giving elements: water.

For further information on these books,
and other titles from Route please visit:

www.route-online.com